*To all faithful preachers, teachers, and Christian leaders
who seek to faithfully expound the Word of God from pulpits or
in Sunday school classes or in home Bible study groups.*

Acknowledgments

I offer all my thanksgiving to the Father in heaven whose Holy Spirit has laid on my heart the writing of this book for the glory of Jesus. I am also immensely grateful to the Lord for sending me an able and gifted editor and compiler of my material in Jim Denney.

Special thanks to the entire team at Harvest House Publishers—and especially to Bob Hawkins Jr. and LaRae Weikert, who shared my vision and made this dream a reality.

My expression of thanks would not be complete without mentioning the patience and perseverance of Don Gates's literary agency for managing the many details of such an undertaking.

My earnest prayer is that, as I leave this legacy to the next generation, God would raise up great men and women to faithfully serve their generation by accurately interpreting the Word of God.

Contents

Introduction

From Rubble to Rejoicing

I f you are dealing with the wreckage of a damaged life, if you feel like an exile living among the ruins of your past, God wants to clear away the rubble and rebuild safe and secure walls of faith in your life. He wants to restore you and empower you to truly live for him.

The Bible is filled with the stories of saints who served God in the midst of trying cirumstances, and they came from a wide variety of vocational callings. Noah was a shipbuilder. Job and Abraham were ranchers with vast herds of livestock. Joseph was a slave who became the prime minister of Egypt. Moses and Joshua were military generals. David was a shepherd, a poet, a warrior, and a king. Deborah was a prophetess and a judge. Matthew was a tax collector and Luke a physician. Paul was a tentmaker and a missionary. And Nehemiah, a cupbearer and trusted advisor to the king of Persia, became God's building contractor.

The name Nehemiah means "the Lord has comforted." He held

one of the most honored positions in the royal city of Susa, in the kingdom of Persia—a position of great prestige, influence, authority, wealth, luxury, and comfort. Though Nehemiah was born in Persia and had never even visited his homeland, Israel, his heart was burdened and broken for that land and for the Jewish people. Though he was raised in a pagan land and served a pagan king, his heart was devoted to the God of Israel. He was a man of pure faith, deep character, and godly leadership.

In the Hebrew Bible, the books of Ezra and Nehemiah were combined as a single book. Ezra tells the story of the rebuilding of the temple in Jerusalem. Nehemiah tells the story of the rebuilding of the walls of Jerusalem. The events of the book of Nehemiah take place soon after the events in Ezra, and Ezra himself appears in the later chapters of the book of Nehemiah.

In the book of Ezra, King Cyrus of Persia is moved by God to issue a decree, permitting the exiled people of Israel to return to Jerusalem. More than 42,000 Jewish exiles, under the leadership of Zerubbabel the governor and Jeshua the high priest, return to the city of Jerusalem. There, under the direction of Ezra the priest, the exiles rebuild the temple. Through the restoration of the temple, Ezra calls the people back to authentic worship and fellowship with God. It's clear that the temple has been rebuilt by the time Nehemiah moves to Jerusalem, because in Nehemiah 6, the pagan opponents of the rebuilding project try to lure Nehemiah into the temple as part of an apparent assassination plot.

Nehemiah, the cupbearer and advisor to the Persian king, emerges as one of the most noble and exemplary leaders in all of Scripture. He is a role model for us all because we are all called to be leaders in some arena of life. In the end, Nehemiah demonstrates that he is far more than a mere building contractor. He shows us how a godly leader prays fervently, makes sound decisions, assembles teams, assigns tasks, faces opposition, manages crises, resolves conflicts, confronts setbacks, and celebrates victory.

I believe God has an important purpose for recording in his Word the story of the rebuilding of the walls. A wall is a powerful symbol. It's more than a simple structure made of stone.

You will recall that, in the book of Joshua, the city of Jericho was surrounded by walls that symbolized the arrogant pride of that pagan city. God demonstrated his power over human arrogance by shattering the walls of Jericho with a mere shout of the Hebrew people—a shout of faith and obedience that invoked God's mighty power. The arrogance of human power is no match for the humble faith of an obedient believer.

Here, in the book of Nehemiah, the walls of Jerusalem symbolize the strength and protection of God in the believer's life. The person who goes through life without faith in God, without a relationship with Jesus Christ, must face the trials, opposition, and setbacks of life without the strong, secure defense that God provides. The story of the rebuilding of the walls of the holy city symbolizes how God stands ready to rebuild the walls of peace and security in any human life, any church, any community, or any nation.

The triumphal account in the book of Nehemiah is the story of how a prayerful, committed believer followed God's leading—then led his people from the rubble of despair to a celebration of rejoicing. You too can go from rubble to rejoicing. Let the book of Nehemiah be your guidebook to a renewed, restored, and reconstructed life.

Turn the page with me—and let the rebuilding begin.

1

The Mighty Power of Prayer

As Saddam Hussein rose to power in Iraq in the late 1960s, he envisioned the restoration of the glories of ancient Babylon. He even planned to rebuild the legendary Hanging Gardens of Babylon, one of the seven wonders of the ancient world. Supremely self-obsessed, Saddam saw himself as the reincarnation of the ancient Babylonian ruler Nebuchadnezzar, and he had ambitions of transforming the nation of Iraq—the former ancient Babylon—into the greatest empire the world had ever seen. He dreamed of uniting the Arab world under his rule.

Saddam Hussein patterned his cruel and bloodthirsty rule after the iron-fisted reign of Nebuchadnezzar. Like Nebuchadnezzar, Saddam placed images and statues of himself all over Iraq. He made sure that even the mildest criticism of his leadership was punished with torture and death. When the Kurds of northern Iraq tried to win their independence in the late 1980s, he responded with a genocidal campaign that may have killed as many as a hundred thousand people, according to Human Rights Watch. He carried out mass slaughter, imprisonment without trial, and grisly torture against untold thousands of his fellow Iraqis. In his ambition to become a new Nebuchadnezzar, Saddam was eager to imitate and exceed (if possible) the worst of Nebuchadnezzar's cruelties.

In the late 1970s, Iraq began construction of a plutonium-producing nuclear reactor with the help of the French government. Saddam Hussein named the reactor Tammuz after the Babylonian month when his ruling Ba'ath party came to power in 1968. Significantly, Tammuz was also the Babylonian month when the armies of King Nebuchadnezzar broke down the walls of Jerusalem in 586 BC, conquering the Jewish capital, suspending the sacrifices in the Jerusalem temple, and resulting in the exile of the Jews to Babylon.

In 1981, threatened by Saddam's growing nuclear threat, Israel dispatched a squadron of seven jets to Iraq. Those jets succeeded in destroying the Tammuz reactor. Though angered by the Israel's destruction of the reactor, Saddam continued building monuments to himself, glorifying himself as the reincarnation of Nebuchadnezzar. He began reconstructing the 600-room palace of Nebuchadnezzar atop the original site. His workers laid more than sixty million bricks atop the original bricks that had been laid in Nebuchadnezzar's time. Each of Saddam's bricks bore the inscription, "To King Nebuchadnezzar in the reign of Saddam Hussein, protector of Iraq, who rebuilt civilization and rebuilt Babylon." Ironically, the bricks inscribed with Saddam's name began to crack within a few years after they were laid.

In March 2003, a US-led international coalition invaded Iraq. Within three weeks of the invasion, the Iraqi government collapsed. For weeks, Saddam Hussein could not be found. Finally, on December 13, American forces found Saddam Hussein, looking filthy, bedraggled, and disoriented. The soldiers pulled him out of the "spider hole" where he had been hiding. On November 5, 2006, after a lengthy trial, Saddam was found guilty of crimes against humanity. He was hanged on December 30.

Saddam dreamed of restoring the glories of Nebuchadnezzar's fabled Babylonian Empire. But Saddam seemed to forget that Nebuchadnezzar suffered his greatest humiliation when he was at the height of his power and glory. The prophet Daniel records that, as Nebuchadnezzar walked along the roof of his royal palace in Babylon (the very palace Saddam attempted to rebuild), he said to himself, "Is not this great Babylon, which I have built by my mighty power as a royal residence and for the glory of my majesty?" (Daniel 4:30).

Even as Nebuchadnezzar boasted, God said to him from heaven: "O King Nebuchadnezzar, to you it is spoken: The kingdom has departed from you, and you shall be driven from among men, and your dwelling shall be with the beasts of the field. And you shall be made to eat grass like an ox, and seven periods of time shall pass over you, until you know that the Most High rules the kingdom of men and gives it to whom he will" (Daniel 4:31-32).

And God's words were immediately fulfilled against Nebuchadnezzar. The king ended up on the ground, eating grass like a beast (see Daniel 4:28-33). Similarly, Saddam—who had pretensions of being the reincarnation of Nebuchadnezzar—ended up living like a beast himself, hiding in a hole under the ground. Instead of rebuilding the Hanging Gardens of Babylon, Saddam found himself hanging from an executioner's noose.

The destruction of Jerusalem

One of King Nebuchadnezzar's achievements—an achievement Saddam Hussain had hoped to repeat—was the conquest of Jerusalem. The original Babylonian conquest of Jerusalem is described in 2 Kings 25.

The Scriptures tell us that King Nebuchadnezzar, in the ninth year of his reign (that is, in January 588 BC), led his army into Judah, surrounded Jerusalem, and laid siege to the city. The Babylonian army built siege works around Jerusalem—temporary structures that included walls, platforms, and towers. The siege works were constructed parallel to the city walls and rose up higher than the walls so that the Babylonian soldiers could shoot arrows down into the city. The siege works probably included scaling ladders, battering rams, and even tunnels under the city walls.

The Babylonians laid siege to the city for a year and a half. During that time, the people of Jerusalem lived in terror. All commerce in and out of the city was stopped, so that the people soon faced the horrors of starvation. The Babylonian archers steadily wore the Jewish people down with sniper attacks from the siege walls.

When the famine was at its height, in the month of Tammuz (approximately our month of July) 586 BC, the army of Nebuchadnezzar breached the city wall. When King Zedekiah of Judah heard that the Babylonians had breached the wall and were pouring into the city, he took his soldiers and escaped by another gate, leaving Jerusalem defenseless. The Babylonians chased King Zedekiah and his army, overtaking them in the plains of Jericho. The soldiers from Judah scattered in terror, abandoning their king. The Babylonians captured King Zedekiah and brought him before Nebuchadnezzar at his battlefield headquarters in Riblah, in modern-day Syria. Nebuchadnezzar cruelly punished King Zedekiah by executing Zedekiah's sons before him, then putting out his eyes so that the death of his sons would be the last sight he would ever see.

Then, at King Nebuchadnezzar's orders, Nebuzaradan, the

captain of Nebuchadnezzar's bodyguard, entered Jerusalem and set fire to the temple of God, to the palace of the king, and to the great houses of the noblemen. The soldiers broke down all the walls that surrounded and protected Jerusalem. Then the Babylonians took the leading citizens of Jerusalem, along with the soldiers who had deserted, and led them off in chains to Babylon. The Babylonians left only the poorest peasants of the land to be farmers and vineyard keepers to grow crops for the benefit of the Babylonian Empire.

The Babylonians stripped the temple of all of its beautiful gold, silver, and bronze furnishings, including all the vessels and implements that were consecrated to the worship of the Lord. They carried these items away into Babylon. The soldiers also took the priests and servants of the Lord's temple and marched them off to Nebuchadnezzar's headquarters in Riblah, and the king himself put them to death.

From 586 to around 430 BC, Jerusalem lay in ruins. The peasants in Judah worked as servants of the Babylonian Empire. Most of the Jews lived in exile and slavery in Babylon. All of the Jews, both the exiles and the ones who were left behind, lived in perpetual despair.

Then God raised up a leader named Nehemiah.

Born in exile, Nehemiah spoke the language of the Persians (by this time, as described in Daniel 5, the Persians had conquered the Babylonian nation). Nehemiah was well-educated in the Persian ways and traditions. As we will see in the last verse of Nehemiah 1, he served as the cupbearer to the king of Persia, Artaxerxes I.

The fact that Nehemiah was a cupbearer doesn't mean he was a waiter. In those days, a cupbearer was the equivalent of the chief of staff, a highly placed advisor to the king. Nehemiah was responsible for the efficient operation of the royal palace at Susa. A man could rise to such a position only by being a hard worker and a person of trustworthy character.

By knowing this one simple fact about Nehemiah—that he was the cupbearer of the king—we immediately know a great deal about Nehemiah's character, his status, his education, and the respect he had earned as an exiled Jew living in Susa. We know that he was a servant, yet he was also a leader and had studied the principles of effective leadership while serving in the court of Artaxerxes. The Jews needed a friend in high places if they ever hoped to rebuild their city and their society.

By God's divine and miraculous appointment, Nehemiah was that man. He would lead the people in rebuilding the walls of the holy city.

Returning from exile and rebuilding their desolate city was the hardest challenge God's people had ever faced. Achieving that goal would require nothing short of a miracle. And in order to experience a miracle in your life, you must be a willing recipient of that miracle. You must be an eager and obedient vessel for God's power.

The walls are broken down

This servant-leader Nehemiah begins his account by telling his own story in the opening lines of Nehemiah 1:

> The words of Nehemiah the son of Hacaliah.

> Now it happened in the month of Chislev, in the twentieth year, as I was in Susa the citadel, that Hanani, one of my brothers, came with certain men from Judah. And I asked them concerning the Jews who escaped, who had survived the exile, and concerning Jerusalem. And they said to me, "The remnant there in the province who had

survived the exile is in great trouble and shame. The wall
of Jerusalem is broken down, and its gates are destroyed
by fire" (1:1-3).

In this scene, some Jewish visitors have come from Judah, so
Nehemiah asks them for news from the homeland, particularly
about the condition of the Jewish capital city, Jerusalem. The visitors tell Nehemiah that Jerusalem is in ruins, its walls and gates
destroyed, and its people suffering from reproach, distress, and
shame.

People respond to bad news in various ways. Some get angry
and put their fist through the wall. Others become depressed and
despondent. But godly people, those who remain in tune with the
Spirit of God, always have one response to bad news: They fall to
their knees in prayer. That was Nehemiah's response:

As soon as I heard these words I sat down and wept
and mourned for days, and I continued fasting and
praying before the God of heaven. And I said, "O LORD
God of heaven, the great and awesome God who keeps
covenant and steadfast love with those who love him
and keep his commandments, let your ear be attentive
and your eyes open, to hear the prayer of your servant
that I now pray before you day and night for the people of
Israel your servants, confessing the sins of the people of
Israel, which we have sinned against you. Even I and my
father's house have sinned. We have acted very corruptly
against you and have not kept the commandments, the
statutes, and the rules that you commanded your servant
Moses. Remember the word that you commanded your
servant Moses, saying, 'If you are unfaithful, I will scatter
you among the peoples, but if you return to me and keep

my commandments and do them, though your outcasts
are in the uttermost parts of heaven, from there I will gather
them and bring them to the place that I have chosen, to
make my name dwell there.' They are your servants and
your people, whom you have redeemed by your great
power and by your strong hand. O Lord, let your ear be
attentive to the prayer of your servant, and to the prayer
of your servants who delight to fear your name, and give
success to your servant today, and grant him mercy in the
sight of this man" (1:4-11).

Nehemiah has received bad news from Jerusalem, and the bad
news has driven him to his knees in prayer. The bad news concerns
the deplorable condition of the people of Jerusalem. But it also concerns the state of the city itself. The walls and gates are destroyed.
The brokenness of Jerusalem's walls is not an insignificant detail. The
meaning of the city's broken walls is extremely important for our
lives today.

The brokenness of the walls signifies the vulnerability and
defenselessness of God's people. It signifies that the people of God
have no protection whatsoever. It's a serious matter when the citizens of a city or a nation are left defenseless and without protection.

Throughout Western civilization, and particularly in America,
we are seeing the protective walls of the culture being systematically
torn down. The abortion laws in America permit the destruction
of life within the womb in every state until the twenty-fourth week,
and in many states all the way through pregnancy. In some states a
woman can walk into an abortion clinic on the day she is scheduled
to deliver her baby, and it is perfectly legal for her to have that baby
put to death (and no, it's not a "fetus," it's a *baby*). Many Americans
don't know that the law allows this, and would even say that I don't

have my facts straight, but this is absolutely true. A nation that willingly, legally permits the slaughter of its children, for any reason or for no reason at all, has chosen to forgo the protection of a just and righteous God.

As we have increasingly permitted the slaughter of children, sacrificing innocent life as an accommodation to our rampant sexual immorality, we have also seen the walls collapse with physician-assisted suicide and the taking of lives (as in the Terri Schiavo case) that some black-robed judge has determined to be without worth. When the life of the child becomes disposable, then the life of a sick, disabled, or aging adult quickly becomes equally disposable.

Our courts and lawmakers have decided that so-called "same-sex marriage" should be legally regarded as the equivalent of traditional marriage—and this is yet another protective wall that is being destroyed. God loves homosexual people in spite of their sin, and so do I—but it is a crime to elevate a same-sex partnership to the equivalence of traditional marriage. One of the many consequences of doing so is that we make it illegal to distinguish between a traditional marriage and a "same-sex marriage" when finding homes for adoptive and foster children. By saying that it doesn't matter if the child has two daddies or two mommies, we are in effect saying that both fathers and mothers are expendable.

Both the Scriptures and child-development experts tell us that, ideally, every child should have a mother and a father. Though it's not always possible for a child to have both parents (for example, if one parent dies), it is a tragic mistake for society to deliberately consign a child to a home in which both parents are either homosexual men or homosexual women. In many ways, I see this as yet another consequence of abortion-on-demand, because society is thinking only of the same-sex couple and their fulfillment and giving no thought whatsoever to what is best for the healthy development of these precious and vulnerable children.

The walls of our culture are falling, and we as citizens are defenseless. The gates of our culture are burned and destroyed, and our children have no protection. As Christians, we have tended to place our faith in the protection of our laws, our government, our borders, our armies, our economy, and our technology. But we are learning that our laws no longer protect us. Our government is turning against us. Our borders are no longer respected. Our armies are stretched to the breaking point. Our economy is built on a shaky foundation and could collapse at any moment. And the technology that was once our servant is fast becoming our master, robbing us of our privacy and freedom.

Though this may sound like a grim diagnosis of our cultural ills, I'm going to surprise you and say that I believe this is a *great* time to be a Christian! Yes, we live in a post-Christian age, but most of what was "Christian" about our society was a mere religious veneer. Yes, our money says, "In God We Trust," but if we are honest with ourselves, our trust has been in our money, not in God.

The walls of our society have fallen. They no longer protect us. We can no longer take comfort behind the walls of our government or our laws or our economy. We can no longer take comfort behind the walls of this political party or that political officeholder. We can no longer take comfort behind marches and movements and methodologies. When the walls have fallen, there's only one way to look— and that is *up*.

These are great days to experience, perhaps for the first time in many years, the powerful hand of God. In times like these, God is able to work miracles. When the walls are crumbling in your life, in your family, in your business, in your world, don't get angry, don't despair. Instead, do what Nehemiah did. Drop to your knees and lift your eyes toward heaven. Then pour out your heart to him in prayer. We like to remain in our comfort zone. We would much rather remain in a condition of indifference and complacency than to be driven to our knees in prayer. But when the walls of safety and security collapse all around us, God is able to get our undivided attention.

As we look around us, we see broken lives and fractured families. People we trusted, people we looked up to as examples of faith and morality, have gotten caught in scandals or have fallen away from the faith. Unbelievers walk past our shattered walls and burned gates, and they mock us and ask, "Where is your God now?"

Tell the mockers to wait—they will see God act. They will see the mighty power of prayer. Because in the calculus of God's universe, there is a simple equation that always proves true: one + prayer = great power. You are that one. God is the great power behind your prayers.

There is a reason you are studying this book right now. God has chosen this time in your life for you to discover the lessons of the life of Nehemiah. All across this land, all across the globe, God is raising up Nehemiahs. He is raising up people who will step up and lead, who will kneel down and pray, who will lift up their eyes to God, who will stand in the gap, and who will help to rebuild the walls of righteousness. God is raising up men and women of Nehemiah-like character and Nehemiah-like faith who will weep in anguish over the broken walls, burned gates, and shattered lives of the people all around. God is raising up people who will lay hold of the mighty power of prayer. God is raising up people who will take him seriously, take him at his word, and spend significant time in the presence of God.

I once heard about a place in Africa where the gospel of Jesus Christ spread like wildfire. Many people came to Christ, and they committed themselves to a daily discipline of prayer. Each believer picked out his or her own private spot outside the village for a quiet time with the Lord. The grasslands and thickets beyond the village became crisscrossed with paths and well-worn spots where people would go to pray.

One interesting benefit of this practice was that every believer could expect his Christian brothers and sisters to literally keep him on the right path. If a believer began to neglect his daily discipline of prayer, a fellow believer would take him aside and hold him accountable, saying, "Brother, the grass grows on your path."

Isn't that a beautiful and gentle way to keep each other on the path of prayer? Are you maintaining a daily discipline of meeting privately with God? Are you experiencing daily the mighty power of prayer? Or has the grass been growing on your path?

The mighty prayer of Nehemiah

God is not impressed with our outward religious display. God wants to do business with men and women who mean business, and who want to be about God's business. How did Nehemiah go about doing God's business?

First, Nehemiah identified the problem. He learned that the city of Jerusalem was desolate, the walls shattered, the gates burned, and the temple in ruins. God's people lived in hopelessness and shame. The very name of the God of Israel was mocked among the pagans. This was the crisis that Nehemiah faced. This was the problem Nehemiah was desperate to solve.

Second, Nehemiah took his problem to the Lord in prayer. He didn't waste time on angry recriminations or blaming others. He fully identified with his people and he acknowledged that he himself was part of the problem. He didn't pray for "their" sins. He came to God confessing, "*We* have sinned against you. Even *I and my father's house* have sinned. *We* have acted very corruptly against you and have not kept the commandments, the statutes, and the rules that you commanded your servant Moses."

Isn't it amazing that Nehemiah took this responsibility upon himself? He could have said, "I feel terrible about the sufferings of my brothers in Jerusalem—but it's really not my problem. I wish I could help, but I have too many duties to attend to right here in Susa." Nehemiah enjoyed wealth, security, and comfort in the court of the king. He had all the privileges any person, Jew or Persian, could ever want. He lived safely and peacefully in Susa. Jerusalem was hundreds of miles away. Why should he get involved in the problems of that city? He had lived all his life in Persia. Just because Judah was his ancestral homeland, why should he get involved in the problems of that distant land?

But that was not Nehemiah's attitude. He identified with his people, who were exiles in Babylon. He longed to restore life and godliness to the land of his forebears, even though he had never seen Judah with his own eyes. He longed to see his people return to the worship of the God of Israel, as commanded by God's servant, Moses. Even though the people were indifferent that day, even though the exiled Jews had conformed themselves to the ways of their captors, Nehemiah longed to see them return to their land, rebuild their walls, and resume their worship of the one true God.

Most important of all, Nehemiah understood that simple spiritual equation: one + prayer = great power. Somehow, Nehemiah grasped the fact that God is not impressed with numbers. God is not intimidated by multitudes. God's judgment is not influenced by majority opinion. One individual plus God is a majority in every situation.

If you truly want to see God at work, then watch him work in a life or a family or a church or a community where the walls are broken, where the gates are shattered, where the people have no hope of rescue but God alone. If you see a man or woman kneel and pray, "Use me, Lord, in this situation, and I will give you all the glory"—then you'd better get out of the way, because great power is coming!

When you read through Nehemiah's prayer, you can see that his heart was broken. But it wasn't the ruined walls that broke Nehemiah's heart. It wasn't the burned gates that broke his heart. It wasn't even that desolate temple that broke Nehemiah's heart. There was only one factor in this entire situation that wounded Nehemiah to the heart: God's name was disgraced. The pagans not only mocked God's people, but they mocked God himself.

The Bible tells us that Nehemiah moaned and wept, fasted and prayed over the sins of his people. When was the last time you wept and fasted over the sins of your nation? When was the last time you prayed in agony over your own sin? When was the last time you sought God in tears over the sin of apostasy in the church? When was the last time you felt genuine anguish at hearing the name of God, the name of his son Jesus, mocked and ridiculed?

Nehemiah experienced agony at the thought of the holy name of Yahweh being ridiculed by the pagans. So he went to his knees and he prayed a threefold prayer. First, he began his prayer with praise. Second, he persisted in prayer. Third, he prepared himself in prayer to do whatever God asked him to do.

Let's take a closer look at the three parts of Nehemiah's prayer.

Part 1: Praise

In verse 4 we hear Nehemiah pray, "O LORD God of heaven, the great and awesome God who keeps covenant and steadfast love with those who love him and keep his commandments." Nehemiah was deeply aware that he stood before the majestic King of the universe. When we pray, we must acknowledge that we stand before an awesome God who deserves our deepest reverence and respect.

Because of Jesus, we can come to him boldly—but not arrogantly. Because of Jesus, we can come to him expectantly—but we must never presume upon his grace. Because of Jesus, we can lay our petitions before him, knowing that he hears our prayers—but we must never make demands on him. Because of Jesus, we can come before God and call him "Abba," meaning "Father" or even "Daddy." We can crawl into his lap and put our arms around him, for he is our heavenly Daddy.

But even an earthly daddy is worthy of respect. Just as a child should never treat his or her daddy with disrespect, we should never treat God as if he were a cosmic bellboy, waiting at our beck and call to do as we demand. Many in the church today seem to have lost their reverence for God. I have heard people make demands on God in prayer, seeming to order him around. Approaching God in prayer without giving him due reverence and respect makes a mockery of prayer.

When we step into the presence of God, we must do so in a spirit of humility and brokenness. If we want God to hear our prayers, then we must approach him prayerfully, not pridefully. The Scriptures tell us that God resists the proud, but he gives grace to the humble. Pride is the antithesis of what God desires from us. Pride is the mortal enemy of prayer. Pride is a hindrance to God's blessings.

If you want to get the glory and the accolades, the praise and the applause, God won't stand in your way. He will let you have all the glory that rightfully belongs to him, if that is what you truly want. But God will cease to use you.

When you try to do God's work *your* way for *your* glorification, you are not going about God's business. You're going about your own business. And if the praise of other people is what you want, you can have it. But don't expect to hear God say to you, "Well done, good and faithful servant." Because that is one thing you have not been. A good and faithful servant does not steal the glory that rightfully belongs to his Master.

Nehemiah went into the presence of God as a man with a broken spirit, a man who confessed his own sinfulness, a man who gave all praise and glory to God alone. We sometimes think of praise as the music we sing in church. But praise is an attitude of the heart, and an attitude of praise transcends all words and all melodies. If our spirit is contrite and broken before God, if we go before him, acknowledging his glory and majesty, then we have hearts full of praise. And the heart that is humble and brimming with praise is a heart that is ready to receive grace from God.

When a little girl named Judy disobeyed, her mother sent her to her room to think about her actions and her attitude. Judy's mother stood outside the little girl's bedroom door and listened as the child first cried, then pouted, then began to pray. "Do you see, God, all the trouble you've gotten me into? Last night I said my prayers and asked you to make me a good girl, and you didn't do it. So it's really all your fault, God, and it's not my fault at all that I was naughty. You didn't answer my prayer, so it's up to you to make Mommy stop being mad at me."

That's a childish prayer, prayed with a childish attitude. Yet it's really not so different from the prayers we adults so often pray. When the choices we make bring bad consequences upon our lives, we are quick to blame circumstances or other people or God himself. We pray, "God, if only my husband wasn't so selfish." Or, "God, if only my wife didn't nag me." Or, "God, if only I had been brought up in a more loving home." Or, "God, if only you hadn't made me to be so easily tempted." And we spend our time in prayer playing the blame game. When we come in prayer with an attitude of shifting blame instead of abject humility and contrition, we are being just as childish as little Judy.

Nehemiah has shown us an example of authentic prayer, mighty prayer, and it begins with humility before our awesome and holy God. As we humble ourselves before God, we recognize that we are completely dependent upon him for our physical well-being, our emotional well-being, our psychological well-being, and our spiritual well-being. There is nothing we have that does not come from him. We are totally dependent on God. And our prayers will have no power until we learn to praise him and recognize our complete dependence on him.

Part 2: Persistence

Nehemiah began his prayer with praise, then he persisted in prayer. He fasted and prayed for a long time. "Pray without ceasing," said the apostle Paul in 1 Thessalonians 5:17. That is the kind of prayer Nehemiah exemplified in this passage.

We see in Nehemiah 1:1 that Nehemiah received the report from the men of Judah in the month of Chislev (approximately November-December on our calendar). As we shall see in Nehemiah 2:1, Nehemiah continued in prayer until the month of Nisan (approximately March-April on our calendar), when he finally took action. So Nehemiah wept over the desolation of Jerusalem and the distress of the Jewish people for about four months. He also wept over his own sins and the sins of his people.

Nehemiah was a prayer warrior. And I don't mean that in a casual sense. Nehemiah went to the battle on his knees. He faced the enemy on his knees. He fought the spiritual forces that were at war with his soul—and he fought them on his knees. He fought them courageously and persistently. His prayer is a great example of spiritual warfare. He refused to yield an inch of ground before his spiritual enemy.

When you pray, do you go to war in prayer? Do you persist in prayer? Do you stand your ground in prayer? Are you truly a warrior in prayer?

The reason we must wage a persistent war in prayer is that there is no cease-fire on the spiritual battlefield. We must keep our spiritual supply lines open so that God can continually give us what we need to continue fighting this war.

Many Christians have the idea that God is reluctant to help us, so we must pray and pray in order to overcome his reluctance and convince him to answer our prayers. But that is not the reality of prayer. God is not reluctant at all. He is eager to bless us. And his chosen means of distributing his blessings is through the power of prayer. When we pray, he showers his bounty upon us. Through prayer, God is able to perform miracles in us and through us.

As the apostle Paul writes, "Now to him who is able to do far more abundantly than all that we ask or think, according to the power at work within us" (Ephesians 3:20). But in order to receive that abundance, we must be about his business. We must be willing to do what he wants, the way he wants it done.

You cannot out-ask God's abundance. You cannot out-imagine God's generosity. There is nothing you can ask of God that he cannot do—so long as you ask him according to his will. So as you pray, be persistent. Persevere in prayer. Continually ask God to conform your will to his. Become God's warrior in prayer. Ask him to align your spirit, your desires, your wants, your yearnings, with his Spirit.

Then watch him do far more in your life then you dare to ask or think.

Part 3: Preparation

Finally, Nehemiah offered a prayer of preparation. It was the prayer of a prepared heart. Nehemiah said, "O LORD, let your ear be attentive to the prayer of your servant, and to the prayer of your servants who delight to fear your name, and give success to your servant today, and grant him mercy in the sight of this man."

Nehemiah identified himself as God's humble servant, and he asked God to give success to him as God's servant, going about God's business. An important principle is at work in Nehemiah's mighty prayer—a principle that you and I should heed: Don't ever ask God for something without having your heart prepared, without being willing to do great things for God.

Prayer is not an excuse for doing nothing. Prayer does not absolve us of the responsibility to act. In fact, if we are going to ask God to pour out his power and blessing on us, we had better be prepared to serve his agenda. When we pray, we must be ready to surrender, to sacrifice, and to serve. As King David once said, "I will not offer burnt offerings to the LORD my God that cost me nothing" (2 Samuel 24:24).

Prayer is not submitting a wish list to God. Prayer is the act of reporting for duty. Prayer is the act of volunteering for service. You and I are God's servants through whom he seeks to accomplish his will. We pray in order to be about God's business.

Nehemiah could have received the report from the Judean visitors, then prayed, "God, bless those people in far-off Jerusalem. If only I could help them myself. But God, you know their need, so please help them with their distress, with their broken walls and shattered gates. O God, please send those people a miracle."

Nehemiah didn't do that. To him, prayer was much more than simply thinking a good thought and sending it to God on behalf of other people. To Nehemiah, prayer was a call to action. Prayer was stepping forward and saying to God, "I'm ready to go. I'm willing to leave the comfort of the palace. I'm willing to step out and risk everything for you and your people. Send me, Lord."

It's one thing to pray, "Lord, please send more workers into the harvest." But it takes a whole different level of commitment, a much deeper level of preparation to pray, "Lord, send *me* into the harvest. Send *me* into my neighborhood, into my workplace, onto my campus, and out into the world to harvest souls for your kingdom."

The prophet Isaiah records the moment when God commissioned him as a prophet to Israel: "And I heard the voice of the LORD saying, 'Whom shall I send, and who will go for us?' Then I said, 'Here I am! Send me'" (Isaiah 6:8). And that is what Nehemiah was saying: Here I am, prayerfully prepared for your service. Send me.

The last sentence of the last verse of Nehemiah 1 is stated very simply, yet the implications of that sentence are profound:

Now I was cupbearer to the king (1:11b).

That simple sentence tells us so much about Nehemiah. We have seen Nehemiah receive a report from the Judean travelers. Then we saw him go down on his knees and pray that mighty prayer of praise, perseverance, and preparation. And now Nehemiah tells us in one sentence about his position: he was the cupbearer to the king. He was God's man in the Persian palace at Susa. He had the ear of the king himself. Nehemiah was strategically placed to be used by God to achieve his purposes in human history.

Nehemiah knew why God had given him such an influential position as cupbearer to the king. So he placed himself completely at the service of the God of Israel. In the rest of this book, we will see how God uses Nehemiah, this fully submitted and obedient servant.

The mighty power of a mother's prayer

Hudson Taylor was born in 1832, the son of a pharmacist father and a mother who was a Methodist lay preacher. His parents raised him in the Christian faith, but he rebelled during his teenage years. He renounced the Christian beliefs of his parents, and he broke his mother's heart. At the age of seventeen, he happened to be in his father's library, looking for a certain book, when he picked up an evangelistic pamphlet titled *Poor Richard*. As he read the pamphlet, he was overwhelmed by the realization of what Jesus Christ had done in dying for him on the cross. Instantly, he dropped to his knees and received Jesus as his Lord and Savior.

At the time, his mother was in another city, about seventy miles away, on church business. When she returned home, about ten days after Hudson's conversion experience, he met her at the door and told her the good news that he had committed his life to Jesus Christ. Strangely, she didn't seem surprised.

"I already know," his mother said.

"But how could you know?" Hudson asked.

"Ten days ago," she said, "on the very day you tell me you read that pamphlet, I rose from the dinner table, and I felt a strong yearning that you should give your life to the Lord Jesus. So I went to my room and I closed the door and turned the key, and I got on my knees and prayed for you. I resolved not to leave that spot until I had God's assurance that my prayers were answered. I pleaded with God in prayer until I could pray no longer. And then I felt his Spirit telling me that all is well. My son has been converted."

Within months of his conversion, Hudson Taylor committed himself to becoming a missionary to China. Before his life was completed, he had spent fifty-one years in China, had founded the China Inland Mission (now OMF International), recruited more than 800 missionaries to the country, founded 125 schools and 300 mission stations in all eighteen provinces of China, and led thousands of Chinese people to the Lord Jesus Christ. He was known not only for his evangelistic passion, but for his great love of the Chinese people and sensitivity to their culture.

And all of this can be traced to the mighty power of a mother's prayer.

What are you praying for? Are you willing to get on your knees and not move from that spot until you feel God's power at work through your prayers?

Through the mighty power of prayer, God makes it possible for us to surrender, to obey, and to be about our Master's business. Prayer calls us to prepare ourselves for service. Through prayer, we can go to God and—like Isaiah, like Nehemiah, like Hudson Taylor—say, "Here I am! Send me."

2

Commitment Ain't Cheap

I n the late 1700s, when William Carey was in his twenties, he became convicted about the Lord's command that we often refer to as the Great Commission: "Go therefore and make disciples of all nations, baptizing them in the name of the Father and of the Son and of the Holy Spirit, teaching them to observe all that I have commanded you" (Matthew 28:19-20a).

Carey traveled around England, speaking in churches, urging Christians to commit themselves to missionary work overseas or to support those who went abroad as missionaries—and he quickly encountered resistance to his message. Many churches in England were gripped by a false doctrine that claimed that Christians do not need to evangelize the world and call sinners to repentance. On one occasion, after Carey spoke at a church, a man told him, "Young man, sit down! When God chooses to convert the heathen, he will do so without your aid and mine."

But William Carey continued preaching about the Great Commission and the cause of world missions. One of his sermons was based on a passage in Isaiah:

> "Enlarge the place of your tent,
>   and let the curtains of your habitations be stretched
>   out;
> do not hold back; lengthen your cords
>   and strengthen your stakes.
> For you will spread abroad to the right and to the left,
>   and your offspring will possess the nations
> and will people the desolate cities."
>   (Isaiah 54:2-3)

There is no surviving transcript of that sermon, but we know that William Carey's message electrified those who heard it. There was one refrain that Carey repeated again and again as he preached—a refrain that imprinted itself on the memories of those who heard it: "Expect great things from God, attempt great things for God, because we have a great God."

That sermon, which became known as the "Deathless Sermon," was the turning point for the missionary movement in England. With that message, William Carey finally broke down all resistance in the church to the missionary effort. Soon, many English believers began training and preparing to launch out into the mission field. Within a few years, Carey founded the organization now known as the Baptist Missionary Society or BMS World Mission. Carey himself went to India, where he translated God's Word into Bengali, Sanskrit, and other languages and dialects.

William Carey's memorable refrain could well serve as the theme for Nehemiah's life: "Expect great things from God, attempt great things for God, because we have a great God." Nehemiah wanted his life to count for God. He was eager to be about the Lord's business and to make a difference for God's kingdom. And Nehemiah also understood that before you can make a difference for God, you have to be a different kind of person than the people around you. Even in the church, unfortunately, very few people are willing to be "different" for God.

Willing to wait

The late pollster George Gallup Jr. was the son of the founder of the Gallup polling organization, and he was a deeply committed Christian. Many of the polls he conducted focused on faith and spirituality in America. Kerby Anderson, founder of Probe Ministries, reported on Gallup's findings about professing Christians in America:

> George Gallup has found that fewer than 10 percent of Americans are deeply committed Christians...Numerous surveys show that most Americans who profess Christianity don't know the basic teachings of the faith. Such shallow spirituality makes them more susceptible to the latest fad, trend, or religious cult. Gallup notes that not being grounded in the faith means that they "are open for anything that comes along." Studies show, for example, that New Age beliefs "are just as strong among traditionally religious people as among those who are not traditionally religious."
>
> Lack of commitment to a faith position and to a lifestyle based upon biblical principles also extends to church attendance and instruction. Eight in ten Americans believe that they can arrive at their own religious views without the help of the church.

Nor is commitment to biblical instruction a high prior-
ity. George Gallup says that Americans are trying to do
the impossible by "being Christians without the Bible."
He adds, "We revere the Bible, but we don't read it." Pastors and pollsters alike have been astounded by the level
of biblical illiteracy in this nation.[1]

Less than 10 percent are willing to stand up with Nehemiah
and say, "Here I am! Send me wherever you will. Use me to make a
difference in my generation for Jesus Christ. Lord, let me be about
your business." Less than 10 percent of people are willing to live
by the motto of William Carey: "Expect great things from God,
attempt great things for God, because we have a great God."

It's important to understand that Nehemiah was not a priest,
not an ordained minister. He had no official position within the
religious structure of the Jewish faith. He was an ordinary layman
who wanted his life to count for God. From the time he received
the report from the men of Judah until he took action was a period
of about four months. He prayed, fasted, wept, and sought God's
will from the month of Chislev to the month of Nisan, from
approximately December to April on our calendar.

Nehemiah didn't rush into things. He spent time in God's
presence, discerning God's will, counting the cost of obedience,
and preparing himself for the challenge ahead. Waiting is often an
important part of preparing ourselves for service to God. When
Jesus commissioned his disciples to preach the gospel to all the world,
he told them to wait until the Holy Spirit had come upon them.

Before you attempt great things for God, you must learn to wait
for God's timing. We become impatient with God's delays—but
God's delay should not be confused with God's denial. When God

says, "Wait," he is not saying, "No." He is telling us, "Be patient. I'm preparing you to attempt great things for my kingdom."

Nehemiah prayed day and night for four months. You and I might have quit by the first month, maybe even the first week. Some Christians seem to think that if they don't have God's answer in the first fifteen minutes, then God must not be in it. We are used to instant gratification. We like fast food from the drive-through window, and our "home-cooked meals" go from freezer to microwave to dinner table in five minutes. So we expect instant results from God. We simply have no patience for waiting on God.

William Carey was a great example of a man of God waiting patiently on the Lord. Before he himself went out to the mission field in India, he spent years in England praying, preaching, and preparing Christians to be supportive of a Great Commission outreach to other lands. He battled prejudice and biblical illiteracy among rigid Christians who had no vision for missionary outreach. Finally, after he preached the Spirit-inspired "Deathless Sermon," the churches of England began sending missionaries out to fulfill the Lord's Great Commission.

But even when William Carey reached the mission field, he labored for seven years, waiting patiently on the Lord, before he finally made his first convert among the Hindus. Imagine laboring for God for seven years without any results to show for it, without a single convert in all that time. William Carey was a patient man, and patience—the willingness to wait for the Lord's timing—is a sign of great spiritual maturity.

Nehemiah was a Jewish man who served the pagan king of Persia. He was living proof of one of the most fundamental of all leadership principles: You cannot lead if you have never followed. You cannot rule if you have never served. You cannot be over if you have never been under. You cannot give if you have never received. You cannot speak to the people if you have never learned to listen.

A true student of leadership, Nehemiah seemed to intuitively understand the leadership lessons Jesus himself would teach nearly five centuries later: If you would save your life, then you must lose it. If you would be great, you must be the servant of all. The way up is down. A true leader is willing to take the towel and the basin and wash the feet of the people he leads. Nehemiah was that kind of leader.

A servant-leader is willing to wait. So Nehemiah waited. He spent four months in prayer before he was able to see God's answer to his prayer.

Facing fear with prayer

During his four months of waiting, Nehemiah experienced deep sadness. He grieved over the suffering of his people and over the sins of his people. The knowledge of the desolation of Jerusalem and the desperation of the Jewish people weighed on Nehemiah's soul.

As he prepared himself in prayer, Nehemiah came to the place of death. He had died to self. He had died to personal ambition. He had died to his sense of security. He had died to his sense of entitlement to be comfortable and successful in Susa. He had died to all of that, and was willing to set aside everything in order to do God's business and serve God's people. The four-month period of preparing himself in prayer was like spending four months at his own funeral.

So it was only natural that the strain, sorrow, and burden that God had laid on his heart would eventually show on his face. His grief had stolen his smile. His burden had caused his countenance to sag. And the king noticed the change that had come over his trusted advisor. Nehemiah records the conversation between himself and King Artaxerxes:

> In the month of Nisan, in the twentieth year of King Artaxerxes, when wine was before him, I took up the wine and gave it to the king. Now I had not been sad in his presence. And the king said to me, "Why is your face sad, seeing you are not sick? This is nothing but sadness of the heart." Then I was very much afraid (2:1-2).

The king asked Nehemiah what was wrong. At that moment, God began to answer the four-month-long prayer of Nehemiah. At last, his opportunity had come and his waiting was over. But notice Nehemiah's response when the king asked why he was so sad: "Then I was very much afraid."

When the king asked Nehemiah what was wrong, his knees began to knock, his heart pounded with fear, his mouth went dry, and his hands shook. If Nehemiah happened to be holding the king's cup at that moment, the royal wine was probably sloshing like ocean waves in a storm. Anyone who claims to attempt great things for God without a sense of fear and trepidation is not being honest.

There's nothing wrong with being afraid. Even heroes experience fear. The difference between a coward and a hero is not that a hero feels no fear, but that a hero won't let fear stampede or paralyze him. A hero is afraid but does his (or her) duty anyway.

Nehemiah was afraid, but he prayed through his fear, and he obeyed God in spite of his fear. He undoubtedly breathed a quick plea to God for help, courage, and strength. Because he had remained in an attitude of prayer for the past four months, the hotline between Nehemiah and the Lord was open, and God's answer came within seconds. The Lord gave Nehemiah the words he should speak:

I said to the king, "Let the king live forever! Why should not my face be sad, when the city, the place of my fathers' graves, lies in ruins, and its gates have been destroyed by fire?" Then the king said to me, "What are you requesting?" So I prayed to the God of heaven. And I said to the king, "If it pleases the king, and if your servant has found favor in your sight, that you send me to Judah, to the city of my fathers' graves, that I may rebuild it." And the king said to me (the queen sitting beside him), "How long will you be gone, and when will you return?" So it pleased the king to send me when I had given him a time. And I said to the king, "If it pleases the king, let letters be given me to the governors of the province Beyond the River, that they may let me pass through until I come to Judah, and a letter to Asaph, the keeper of the king's forest, that he may give me timber to make beams for the gates of the fortress of the temple, and for the wall of the city, and for the house that I shall occupy." And the king granted me what I asked, for the good hand of my God was upon me (2:3-8).

Why was Nehemiah so afraid? The answer can be found in Ezra 4. There we see that Cyrus, king of Persia from 559 to 530 BC, had previously given an order to rebuild the temple of Jerusalem. Years passed, and certain enemies of the Jewish people wrote a letter to a later Persian king, saying, "The Jews who came up from you to us have gone to Jerusalem. They are rebuilding that rebellious and wicked city…They will not pay tribute, custom, or toll, and the royal revenue will be impaired" (see Ezra 4:12-13). In response, the king ordered that all work on the temple in Jerusalem should immediately stop. So the work of rebuilding was thwarted. As we see in the book of Daniel, once the king issues an order, it cannot be revoked, according to the law of the Medes and Persians (see Daniel 6:8,12,15).

So Nehemiah was afraid to speak up to King Artaxerxes because he was asking the king to do what was unlawful according to the law of the Medes and Persians. He was asking the king to revoke the earlier order and to order the rebuilding to proceed once more. No wonder Nehemiah was shaking in his boots! No wonder Nehemiah said, "I prayed to the God of heaven" before making his request to the king. Nehemiah was risking execution to even suggest such a notion.

But Nehemiah obeyed God, not his fears. He made his request to the king: "If it pleases the king, and if your servant has found favor in your sight, that you send me to Judah, to the city of my fathers' graves, that I may rebuild it."

Nehemiah's bold request

What did Nehemiah ask the king for? He said, in effect, "Your majesty, I need some time off. I want a leave of absence with full pay. And I want you to give me a decree ordering the rebuilding of the city and its walls. But that's not all. I want your personal Secret Service detail to go along with me for protection. And there's more. I want you to give me a purchase order on the king's credit card so that I can buy all the timber we will need to reconstruct the city gates, the city buildings, and even the house I will live in during the reconstruction."

The king had to be impressed with Nehemiah's audacity. He was not only asking King Artaxerxes to countermand his former order, in violation of the law of the Medes and Persians, but he was even asking for King Artaxerxes to finance the whole project.

Where did Nehemiah acquire the chutzpah to make such a bold

request of the king? It came from the Spirit of God during Nehemiah's four months of prayer, fasting, and weeping. When Nehemiah was praying, he wasn't doing all the talking. He was also listening. He received detailed plans for what God wanted him to accomplish, plans for the rebuilding of the city and the temple. And those plans included the fact that God intended for King Artaxerxes to finance the reconstruction of Jerusalem.

I believe King Artaxerxes was honored by the boldness of Nehemiah's request. In fact, I believe Nehemiah's bold request is intended to teach us something about prayer. The way Nehemiah approached King Artaxerxes and presented his requests is precisely the way we are to approach God and present our requests to him. Nehemiah was not timid, and the request he made was breathtaking in its boldness and expense. Nehemiah dared to ask the king to provide resources that, in today's terms, would be worth millions of dollars.

Was the king affronted or offended? No! He was honored because Nehemiah actually gave praise and glory to the king by making such a bold request. By asking the king to provide him with services and materials worth millions of dollars, Nehemiah acknowledged the vast scope of the king's power and the endless extent of the king's resources. He even honored the king by presenting him with a seemingly impossible challenge. In order for the king to grant Nehemiah's request, the king would have to revoke a previous royal order, an act that would violate the law of the Medes and Persians.

Our king is the King of heaven. He has all the resources of the universe at his disposal. When we go to him with bold and audacious requests, daring to ask him to do the impossible and to lavish his resources upon us, we actually glorify, honor, and please him. If we pray halfheartedly and timidly, if we dare to ask only for a few crumbs of his grace, we do not honor God, we insult him. It's as if we are saying, "God, I know your power is limited. I know your resources are finite. I don't want to ask too much of you, because I know your blessings are very tightly budgeted. But if you could spare me just half a blessing, I'd really appreciate it."

It sounds ridiculous, but aren't many of our prayers just like that? God is waiting for his children to come to him with a truly bold request. When one of his children kneels to pray, I can see the Lord saying to his angels, "Get ready, boys. This may be the prayer request of the century!"

But it usually turns out to be a fainthearted saint with a half-hearted prayer. So the Lord hears the prayer, then turns to the angels and says, "Never mind. As you were."

Nehemiah was bold. He asked the king for security and safety, for the protection of horsemen and soldiers, for a lavish amount of timber for construction. Nehemiah's request was so daring that his knees knocked and his hands shook as he spoke.

In our prayers to God, do we dare to ask God for the impossible? Do we boldly ask him to do the unthinkable? Do our knees knock and our hands shake as we present our immense, unrestrained, unflinching requests before our infinite God?

Remember, this is the God whom the apostle Paul describes in these words: "Now to him who is able to do far more abundantly than all that we ask or think, according to the power at work within us, to him be glory in the church and in Christ Jesus throughout all generations, forever and ever. Amen" (Ephesians 3:20-21).

If our God is able to do exceedingly, abundantly more than we can even think or ask, then why do we approach him so timidly with our feeble little requests? Why don't we come boldly before his throne of grace, asking him to pour out the blessings of heaven onto our lives, asking him to empower us to dare great things for his kingdom? When we pray according to God's will, he will give us more than we asked for, more than we dare to imagine.

Notice the last sentence in verse 8: "And the king granted me what I asked, for the good hand of my God was upon me." Nehemiah presented his request to the king—and King Artaxerxes granted the request. But notice who gets the credit and the glory. It's not Nehemiah. It's not even the king. Nehemiah said, "The good hand of my God was upon me." The Lord gets the glory.

Nehemiah did not boast about his boldness in presenting his request to the king. And Nehemiah did not give glory to the king for granting his request. He gave glory to God. You might say that Nehemiah bragged on God. When God showers his blessings onto your life, when he answers your prayers in a powerful way, do you brag on God? Do you tell your friends, "Look at the amazing thing God did in my life"? Do you give God the glory he deserves?

Nehemiah spent four months in prayer, talking to God and listening to God. He needed every ounce of courage he could summon in order to present his bold request to the king. At the end of that time of fasting and prayer, he made his request to the king. Because God's hand was with Nehemiah, the king gave Nehemiah everything he requested. But Nehemiah was about to find out that the challenges ahead were going to get harder, not easier. He was about to discover that commitment ain't cheap.

Surveying the devastation

Next, Nehemiah travels to Jerusalem—and we immediately see opposition brewing:

> Then I came to the governors of the province Beyond the River and gave them the king's letters. Now the king had sent with me officers of the army and horsemen. But when

Sanballat the Horonite and Tobiah the Ammonite servant heard this, it displeased them greatly that someone had come to seek the welfare of the people of Israel.

So I went to Jerusalem and was there three days. Then I arose in the night, I and a few men with me. And I told no one what my God had put into my heart to do for Jerusalem. There was no animal with me but the one on which I rode. I went out by night by the Valley Gate to the Dragon Spring and to the Dung Gate, and I inspected the walls of Jerusalem that were broken down and its gates that had been destroyed by fire. Then I went on to the Fountain Gate and to the King's Pool, but there was no room for the animal that was under me to pass. Then I went up in the night by the valley and inspected the wall, and I turned back and entered by the Valley Gate, and so returned. And the officials did not know where I had gone or what I was doing, and I had not yet told the Jews, the priests, the nobles, the officials, and the rest who were to do the work.

Then I said to them, "You see the trouble we are in, how Jerusalem lies in ruins with its gates burned. Come, let us build the wall of Jerusalem, that we may no longer suffer derision." And I told them of the hand of my God that had been upon me for good, and also of the words that the king had spoken to me. And they said, "Let us rise up and build." So they strengthened their hands for the good work (Nehemiah 2:9-18).

People often look at people in leadership and think, *What a cushy job that person has!* or, *If I had that job, I'd be a much better leader.* Leadership looks easy from the outside. Only those who are actually sitting on the leadership hot seat know about the personal cost involved in being a leader—the stress and anxiety, the problems to be solved, the decisions to be made, the opposition and criticism to be endured, the obstacles to overcome, the weight of responsibility.

In these verses we meet two men, soon to become Nehemiah's worst enemies. Sanballat the Horonite and Tobiah the Ammonite are stirred up against Nehemiah even before he arrives in Jerusalem. These men are pagans and bigots who demonstrate an unreasoning hatred toward the Jewish people.

Nehemiah arrived in Jerusalem but kept his presence there a secret. After three days, he arose at night, accompanied by a few men for protection. He went around the city, inspecting the walls and gates[2] and assessing the work that needed to be done to rebuild the city. No one knew Nehemiah's business there because he had not yet spoken to the Jewish people, the priests, the nobles, the officials, and others who would have to do the work of rebuilding Jerusalem and its walls.

The people God raises up as leaders must be willing to endure the suffering of solitude. Those whom God commissions for his work must often begin their days in isolation and end their days in lonely reflection. In solitude, they must commune with God, listening to his plan, before they can go out and serve his people. They must agonize in private with God before they can stand in front of the people to lead them. They must hear the voice of God in the silence of their thoughts before they can go out and speak for him.

I have found this principle to hold true in my own life as a minister of the gospel. For every minute I spend preaching to the congregation, I must spend at least an hour in solitude with God. If I did not spend significant time alone with God, if I spent my week engaged in busy pursuits, I would not have a word to bring from the Lord.

Nehemiah was committed to God and commissioned by God, and he faced an overwhelming task. The weight of the responsibility of resurrecting the city of Jerusalem from the dust and rubble of its desolation must have been almost unbearable. While all of Judah slept, Nehemiah was awake. He was inspecting, studying, surveying, probing, and praying.

Nehemiah is a role model to us all. He is a role model of prayer. He is a role model of leadership. He is a role model of the kind of godly leader who truly listens to God, who takes his orders from God, who endures the isolation of waiting patiently in the shadows with God—waiting for God's chosen time to act. And when Nehemiah's time finally comes, he acts courageously and without hesitation, rejecting his fears, stepping out of his comfort zone, obediently following God's call, accepting the lonely challenge of leadership.

"Let us rise up and build"

All of us are called to be leaders in some arena of life. If nothing else, you are a leader in your home. And you are probably also a leader in some other arena—on your campus, in your church, in your office, in your ministry, in your military unit, or in your civic organization. God has called you to be a leader in some aspect of your life. He has equipped you with gifts for leadership and serving. As a leader, you must be prepared to spend time alone with God, listening to him, allowing yourself to be prepared and trained and commissioned by him to step out and lead.

As we look around us, it is painfully obvious that the walls are breaking down. The walls of our culture have crumbled. The walls of the church are in ruins. The walls of our families are broken down. God is calling us to be the Nehemiahs of our time. He is calling us to step up and lead in a time that is bereft of leadership.

The walls of our cities are broken. Violent crime is rampant. Our neighborhoods are war zones. Lawlessness is everywhere. Do we care about the broken walls and burned gates of our own cities?

We need to walk around the broken walls and shattered gates of our education system, from our public schools to our universities. In many cases, if we knew what was really being taught to our young people, we would be heartbroken, even horrified. We send our children off to learn to read, write, think, and understand their history, their government, and their place in the world. Instead, they are taught to detest their country and to deny their faith. Instead of being taught how to succeed and lead in life, they are indoctrinated in "political correctness" and notions of "safe sex." They are taught to despise the Founding Fathers and distrust the Constitution. The walls of our educational institutions are shattered, our children are left defenseless, and most parents don't even know it.

The protective enclosure of our moral walls and spiritual gates has been turned to rubble. The vast majority of churchgoing people have no higher moral standards than the unchurched people around them. As George Gallup's research has shown, less than a tenth of Americans are deeply committed Christians. Most professing Christians are biblically illiterate and wide open to any worldly philosophy that comes along. No wonder the walls of morality have fallen. No wonder the church, like the surrounding culture, is ravaged by the breakdown of the family, increasing adultery, domestic violence, and child abuse. And when the walls of the family are broken, the foundation of society has collapsed.

One of the most pervasive signs of moral brokenness in the church today is the rise of personal indebtedness. Indiscriminate buying on credit is a symptom of the sin of greed and covetousness. We want what we want, and we want it now. We are no longer able to distinguish between necessities and luxuries, so we think we have to have that expensive new car, that mansion-sized house, that sailboat, that theater-sized 3-D television—and all of it bought on credit. Many Christians are so deep in debt that they cannot possibly pay their tithes and offerings to the Lord. When you are unable to meet your financial obligations to God, you are in financial bondage. The walls of your financial life are broken and need to be rebuilt.

We need Christian men and women who are willing to spend time on their knees, alone with God, listening to his leading. Then, after spending significant time on their knees, those Christian leaders need to rise up and say, "Enough is enough!" We need Christian men and women who will boldly stand up to the powers that be, who will run for office and take positions of leadership on boards of education, on university boards, on county and city boards, and at various levels of state and federal government. We need a new generation of Nehemiahs who are willing to be God's people in our time, surveying the ruins of our society, then planning and engineering the moral and spiritual reconstruction of our society.

Institutional Christianity has failed. But we should never confuse institutional Christianity with biblical Christianity. While the surrounding culture is littered with the rubble of moral relativism, the truth of God's Word stands firm as the only secure wall against cultural decay and decline. While the walls of our culture have fallen, the walls of our faith remain secure.

As we survey the wreckage of our culture, much as Nehemiah surveyed the wreckage of Jerusalem, it would be easy for us to feel overwhelmed and discouraged by the enormity of the task. But like Nehemiah, we serve a God who is greater than all the powers of this world. Nehemiah is our role model, our example for how we must go about the work of rebuilding our broken world.

How did Nehemiah begin rebuilding the walls of Jerusalem? After surveying the task, he delivered a message to the people: "You see the trouble we are in, how Jerusalem lies in ruins with its gates burned. Come, let us build the wall of Jerusalem, that we may no longer suffer derision." He also told the people that the hand of God was upon him and that King Artaxerxes had given his approval and support to their project.

Nehemiah writes that, as a result of his words of encouragement, the people "strengthened their hands for the good work." Notice that Nehemiah did not say, "You must build the wall of Jerusalem." He said, "Come, let *us* build the wall of Jerusalem." Spoken like a true leader. Nehemiah reminds me of the wise words of department store magnate Harry Gordon Selfridge:

> The boss drives people; the leader coaches them.
> The boss depends on authority; the leader on
>   goodwill.
> The boss says 'I'; the leader says 'We.'
> The boss fixes the blame for the breakdown; the leader
>   fixes the breakdown.
> The boss knows how it is done; the leader shows how.
> The boss says, 'Go'; the leader says, 'Let's go!'"[3]

Nehemiah was a leader not a boss. He didn't say, "Go." He said, "Let's go!" He identified with the people he led. He used phrases such as "the trouble *we* are in" and "let *us* build the wall" and "that *we* may no longer suffer derision." He did not shout orders from an ivory tower. He got down in the trenches with his people.

Constructionists and obstructionists

In verse 10, we were introduced to a pair of villains, two antagonists who will oppose Nehemiah's leadership and his effort to rebuild Jerusalem: "But when Sanballat the Horonite and Tobiah the Ammonite servant heard this, it displeased them greatly that someone had come to seek the welfare of the people of Israel." At the end of Nehemiah 2, we meet them again, along with a third man, Geshem the Arab:

> But when Sanballat the Horonite and Tobiah the Ammonite servant and Geshem the Arab heard of it, they jeered at us and despised us and said, "What is this thing that you are doing? Are you rebelling against the king?" Then I replied to them, "The God of heaven will make us prosper, and we his servants will arise and build, but you have no portion or right or claim in Jerusalem" (2:19-20).

Nehemiah's opponents are no different from many scoffers and antagonists in our time. The moment they hear that God is doing a great work, they oppose it. They obstruct it. They mock and ridicule the builders. When godly people try to raise something up, they can't wait to tear it down.

There are two kinds of people in the world—the constructionists and the obstructionists. Which kind are you? Do you prefer to build or to tear down? Do you seek to encourage or to discourage? Do you seek to spread faith and optimism—or do you prefer to spread gloom and doom?

If you are a builder, a constructionist, and you are determined to dare something great for God, then you can expect opposition. You can expect people to criticize you, mock you, and attempt to undermine you with innuendos and false accusations. Sanballat, Tobiah, and Geshem played the obstructionist role in the life of Nehemiah, and if you are attempting great things for God, you can probably think of people who play this same obstructionist role in your life today.

You can find Sanballats, Tobiahs, and Geshems in every community, in every organization, and yes, you can find them in the church. It's important to note in verse 20 how Nehemiah responds to the obstructionists in his life: "The God of heaven will make us prosper, and we his servants will arise and build, but you have no portion or right or claim in Jerusalem."

Nehemiah's reply is confident, assertive, and direct. He tells these opponents that God will give them success, that the people will build the walls, they will not be deterred by opposition, and those who oppose God's work will have no part in the blessings of the restored city.

It was essentially the same message that Lee Iacocca delivered in an advertising campaign when he was chairman of the Chrysler Corporation, "Lead, follow, or get out of the way." Or as the apostle Paul said, "If God is for us, who can be against us?" (Romans 8:31b). Or as Jesus himself said, "On this rock I will build my church, and the gates of hell shall not prevail against it" (Matthew 16:18b).

We are all called to be leaders in some arena of life. We are all called by God to be builders and constructionists. The example of Nehemiah teaches us that it is vitally important that we spend significant time on our knees, talking to God and listening to God. And when he calls us to action, we must summon our courage and faith, and we must step up and lead. We can go forth, expecting great things from God, attempting great things for God, because we have a great God.

Opposition does not intimidate us. Obstructionists do not stop us. God has called us, so we are confident. The God of heaven will make us successful. He will see us through.

3

The Body Needs Everybody

n John 5, Jesus healed a paralyzed man at the pool of Bethesda in Jerusalem. John tells us the pool was located by the Sheep Gate. Jesus would later pass through the Sheep Gate, bleeding and disfigured, bearing the cross on his shoulders, as the Roman soldiers led him out of the city to be crucified. Though the Scriptures do not specifically tell us that Jesus passed through the Sheep Gate, we do know that this is the gate that led to Golgotha, the place of crucifixion.

It's significant that Jesus had to pass through the Sheep Gate on his way to the hill where he would be sacrificed. That gate was called the Sheep Gate for one all-important reason: Over the centuries, thousands and thousands of sheep and lambs had passed through that gate on their way to the temple to be sacrificed for the sins of the people. All of those sacrificial sheep and lambs symbolically represented Jesus, the perfect and sinless Lamb of God, who passed through that very gate on his way to be sacrificed for the sins of the world.

Like the paralyzed man at the pool of Bethesda, our healing begins at the Sheep Gate. Our salvation begins at the Sheep Gate. Our relationship with God begins with the shed blood of the perfect Lamb. And as we will see here in Nehemiah 3, the rebuilding of our broken lives symbolically begins at the Sheep Gate. For it is at the Sheep Gate that Nehemiah begins the reconstruction of the walls of Jerusalem.

Three leadership lessons

We have seen that Nehemiah is a role model of prayer, courage, leadership, and obedience to God's will. Now we will see Nehemiah in action, leading the rebuilding of the walls of Jerusalem. He exemplifies one of the key principles of good leadership, which is taking a large and daunting task—rebuilding the ruined walls of an entire city—breaking that huge task into a lot of smaller tasks, and delegating those smaller tasks to teams of people. This leadership principle is a key to the effective, healthy functioning of any group of people, from a family to a sports team to an organization to a nation.

As you open your Bible to Nehemiah 3, your first reaction might be, "Oh no, this looks like one of those Bible genealogies—a lot of characters but very little plot." I can understand that reaction, but I think a closer examination will reveal some deep truths for our lives. In fact, Nehemiah 3 is the very heart of the book of Nehemiah.

This chapter reveals God's strategy for rebuilding a city wall, for rebuilding a church, and for rebuilding our lives. Once we begin to understand and accept God's strategy for our lives, once we begin to understand the work he is doing through us, life becomes exciting. Life becomes an adventure. The moment we see God working out his strategy in our lives, we have a reason to jump out of bed every morning with enthusiasm and energy. Knowing that the Almighty God of the universe is working out his eternal plan through our lives gives us a real passion and zest for living.

As we examine how Nehemiah leads the people in rebuilding the walls, we will see God's strategy for our lives today. We notice first of all that Nehemiah was a realist. He carefully surveyed the walls of Jerusalem, and he clearly understood the enormity of the task. He had no intention of attempting this task alone or even with a small core of professional engineers. In order to rebuild the walls of Jerusalem within a reasonable time—less than two months—he had to summon the strength and skills of the entire population of the city. He had to motivate and mobilize *all* the people to rise up and rebuild.

Everyone had to take ownership of the project. Everyone had to take pride in the work of rebuilding. Everyone had to be willing to accept Nehemiah's authority, put aside any differences they might have with their neighbors, and work side by side to achieve a single goal.

In this chapter, we see three lessons in effective leadership that are as valid today as they were in Nehemiah's time. Without these three principles, a leader can accomplish nothing. But if an entire organization operates by these three principles, a leader can accomplish almost anything. Those three principles are:

1. Consolidation

2. Cooperation

3. Confirmation

Let's look at each of these principles in turn.

Principle 1: Consolidation

Rather than include the entire text of Nehemiah 3 here, I want to focus on the phrases that repeat in the chapter, because these patterns are important to understanding the meaning of Nehemiah 3. In the opening verses, we read:

> Then Eliashib the high priest rose up with his brothers the priests, and they built the Sheep Gate. They consecrated it and set its doors. They consecrated it as far as the Tower of the Hundred, as far as the Tower of Hananel. And next to him the men of Jericho built. And next to them Zaccur the son of Imri built (3:1-2).

Note the phrases "next to him" and "next to them." "Next to" appears fifteen times in Nehemiah 3. In the original Hebrew, that phrase literally means "at their hands." Nehemiah had divided the people into groups, and he stationed those groups at the different gates around the city. These groups of people were arranged in such a way that they were next to each other, literally at the hand of each other, within easy reach of each other. Where one group of builders left off, another began. The entire perimeter of the city was ringed with builders, each responsible for one section of the wall.

This is the principle of *consolidation*. To consolidate is to bring together many separate parts into a single unified whole. Nehemiah consolidated all the faithful people of Jerusalem and the surrounding region into a single unified force for rebuilding the city. Once he had consolidated the people, he organized and arranged them so they would work side by side, hand by hand, leaving no gap between them.

There is a lesson in this for you and me. Paul tells us that we are fellow workers and fellow laborers with God (see 1 Corinthians 16:16; 1 Thessalonians 5:12; 1 Timothy 5:17). Jesus is building and consolidating his church with our hands. When we do God's work, when we build together as Christians, we must stand side by side and hand by hand, leaving no gap between us. This does not mean that we necessarily agree with each other on every issue, but it does mean that we love each other, accept each other, and cooperate with each other. We must never forget that we are colaborers with Christ, and we are working as a consolidated force, building together under the direction and leadership of God.

Nehemiah 3 lists thirty-eight names and forty-two groups. There is an amazing diversity, and each group is assigned to a certain section of the wall or a certain gate for a reason. Eliashib the high priest and his fellow priests were chosen to rebuild the Sheep Gate because that is the gate through which the people brought the sheep and lambs that the priests would sacrifice to the Lord. The high priest was doing gritty, strenuous manual labor right alongside the lowly temple servants. You don't usually see priests trading their vestments for a pair of overalls and the implements of stonemasonry—but these were unusual times.

In this passage, we see powerful politicians working alongside merchants and craftspeople, stonemasons and carpenters, potters and cloth weavers, goldsmiths and perfumers. We see not only men but women laboring in the hot sun to rebuild the walls of Jerusalem. One man, the ruler of half the district of Jerusalem, is working alongside his daughters. Perhaps some of the single women figured out that a construction site was a good place to meet strong, brawny, marriageable men.

Workers came from the region around Jerusalem, from the towns and districts of Jericho, Tekoa (home of the Tekoites), Gibeon, Mizpah, Beth-zur, and Keilah. Some of the laborers worked quickly, completed their section, and then moved to another section of the wall, eagerly shouldering an extra share of the workload. But there are also slackers among them. Though the blue-collar Tekoite workers were happy to pitch in and work hard, the noblemen from Tekoa, Nehemiah writes, "would not stoop to serve their Lord" (3:5). We see this same dichotomy in the church today—hardworking, good-hearted Christians who are eager to serve the Lord and serve others in any way they can, plus a number of stuffed shirts who prefer to sit and watch others work but would never think of getting a little dirt under their fingernails.

The church needs as many average, ordinary, hardworking Tekoites as possible—but the church is unfortunately oversupplied with self-important, uninvolved Tekoite nobles. The self-appointed nobles in the church are seldom shy about offering criticism, but offer them a job to do and see how quickly they disappear! The Tekoite nobles among us are eager to share in the victories, but not in the battles. They want to participate in the celebration, but not in the grunt work.

Jesus did not build his church to be an arena for spectators. He has called us all to the playing field. We are all part of the same team. He has consolidated us into a single united force for change. In the church of Jesus Christ, there is plenty of room for both priests and servants, political leaders and tradesmen, old men, young men, old women, young women. The only people there is no room for are those who are too prideful and arrogant to do the Lord's work.

The work Jesus has given to his church is not easy. Our job is nothing less than rebuilding the walls of our culture, the walls of our church, and the walls of broken lives around us. In our community and neighborhoods, people are dying apart from Christ. They are headed for the judgment of God, and they will face God alone and stained with sin unless they respond to the invitation of the Lord

Jesus Christ. We have the message of eternal life. We have the job of sharing the good news of salvation with those who are lost.

You and I have to ask ourselves, "If every member of the church were just like me, what kind of church would it be? If everyone in our church shared Christ as often as I share Christ, how many people would come to know the Lord? If everyone in our church attended the way I attend, gave the way I give, and worked the way I work, what kind of church would it be? Would it be a vibrant, growing church filled with new believers? Or would it be a dead institution, spiritually and even financially bankrupt?"

The principle of consolidation is the secret of a vibrant, growing church. God has consolidated all of us together within the church, the body of Christ—not to assemble a crowd of spectators but to assemble an army that will move out onto the spiritual battlefield and take territory in the name of King Jesus. Are you living by the principle of consolidation?

Principle 2: Cooperation

The second leadership lesson in Nehemiah 3 is cooperation. Nehemiah exemplified the first lesson, consolidation, when he brought people together from their various places, their various backgrounds, with their various skills, and unified them into a single force for rebuilding the city of Jerusalem. But Nehemiah also exemplified the importance of cooperation in any organizational activity.

The people who lined up side by side and hand by hand all around the perimeter of the city were a highly diverse collection of people. In any organization, you have a lot of different personality types. Some are self-starters; others need to be told what to do and how to do it. Some are natural leaders; others are natural followers.

Some are talkative extroverts; others are quiet introverts. Some are energetic and impatient; others are steady and easygoing. Nehemiah undoubtedly saw the whole range of personality types represented in his reconstruction team.

Personality differences easily lead to clashes and conflict, so Nehemiah had to make sure that his team's diversity was a strength, not a weakness. Wherever you see diversity without unity you find suspicion and division, leading to a breakdown of the organization. But wherever you see a great diversity of skills, gifts, and personality types expressed in a spirit of mutual love, acceptance, and unity, you will see an incredible work being accomplished.

This is a picture of how the Lord Jesus intends his church to function. We recognize our different gifts and personalities, yet we are united in our purpose and our obedience to the Master. Every member plays an integral part. We don't all perform the same task in the same place. Every member works at his or her own task at his or her own position—but every member, every task, every position is indispensable. We all need each other, and we all serve the same Master. The apostle Paul explained the cooperation principle this way:

> Now there are varieties of gifts, but the same Spirit; and there are varieties of service, but the same Lord; and there are varieties of activities, but it is the same God who empowers them all in everyone...
>
> The eye cannot say to the hand, "I have no need of you," nor again the head to the feet, "I have no need of you." On the contrary, the parts of the body that seem to be weaker are indispensable, and on those parts of the body that we think less honorable we bestow the greater honor, and our unpresentable parts are treated

with greater modesty, which our more presentable parts do not require. But God has so composed the body, giving greater honor to the part that lacked it, that there may be no division in the body, but that the members may have the same care for one another (1 Corinthians 12:4-6,21-25).

Nehemiah's reconstruction team possessed this high degree of diversity that Paul talks about. Because the people possessed a great diversity of skills, Nehemiah could match them to a wide range of tasks that needed to be accomplished. Nehemiah directed that some should serve as foremen and overseers, others should remove debris, others should mix mortar, others should chisel and shape stones, and still others should lay and fit the stones for the wall.

Unfortunately, as Nehemiah tells us in this passage, some thought their job was to sit and watch the others work. These were the so-called nobles, but for the life of me, I can't understand what is noble about sitting back in the shade, sipping cold lemonade, while others are working in the hot sun. Sooner or later, the people who are working hard will need to be relieved. The work must go on, but if the nobles don't get off their duffs and lend a hand, the other workers will inevitably suffer exhaustion and burnout.

Years ago, the syndicated columnist Ann Landers quoted an unknown author who wrote these penetrating words about the need for cooperation:

> This is a story about four people: Everybody, Somebody, Anybody, and Nobody. There was an important job to be done and Everybody was asked to do it. Everybody was sure Somebody would do it. Anybody could have done it but Nobody did it. Somebody got angry about that because it was Everybody's job. Everybody thought

Anybody could do it but Nobody realized that Everybody wouldn't do it. It ended up that Everybody blamed
Somebody when actually Nobody asked Anybody.[4]

This is a syndrome that afflicts the church today just as it afflicted
the lazy "nobles" during the rebuilding of the walls of Jerusalem.

In this chapter, Nehemiah lists only the heads of the households
that took part in the rebuilding. In that culture, families were very
large, so a vast number of people actually worked on the walls. Their
individual names are not listed nor are their specific tasks. That
information is lost to history—but it is not lost to God. He knows
what every man and woman did to rebuild the walls and resurrect
Jerusalem from its rubble and ashes.

In the same way, people may not notice all that you do to serve
God and others. People may not notice the work you contribute to
the church, the sacrifices you make to meet needs and to help spread
the gospel. But God knows, and he does not forget.

As the Scriptures remind us, "For God is not unjust so as to over-
look your work and the love that you have shown for his name in
serving the saints, as you still do" (Hebrews 6:10). God is just. God
knows your heart and he knows your work and the quiet and humble ministry you are doing in his name. Your service to God may
not make headlines on earth, but it does make headlines in heaven.

Unfortunately, the church today has no shortage of people who
have never learned to cooperate. They don't seem to understand
the biblical imperative of Christian unity and Christian love. They
major on the minor issues and minor on the major issues. They
concentrate on what matters to their spiritual pride and ignore
what is important to the kingdom and the heart of God. When
some people are building while others are tearing down, the church
becomes paralyzed, dysfunctional, and ineffective.

The example of Nehemiah and the rebuilding of the walls of Jerusalem is a vivid example of how the church should function. As we seek to rebuild the walls of the church, we need to stand side by side, leaving no gap between us, cooperating together, building together, and serving together so that one day we may celebrate what we have built together.

The enemy of our unity is the flesh, our sin nature, our self-centeredness. In the flesh, we focus on how right we are and how wrong others are. Instead of focusing on our unity in the church, the body of Christ, we focus on the petty issues that divide us. God does not expect us to always agree with one another, but he does expect us to love one another, accept one another, and forgive one another. We will always have different points of view on various issues. We can't help having personality clashes from time to time. But our love for the Lord Jesus requires us to maintain our unity in the Holy Spirit. That's what true Christian fellowship is all about.

CBS news commentator Charles Osgood told the story of two women who lived in a nursing home. Both women had been accomplished pianists in their younger years, but each had suffered a debilitating stroke and had given up all hope of ever playing the piano again. One woman, Margaret, suffered paralysis on her left side; the other woman, Ruth, suffered paralysis on her right side.

The director of the nursing home learned from family members about the musical accomplishments of both Margaret and Ruth—and he had an idea. He went to the two women and suggested that they sit down at the piano and see what they could accomplish by working together. So Margaret and Ruth tried working together on a musical piece. Their first attempts were frustrating and unsuccessful. Both women were ready to quit—when they found a song they could play together, each supplying one hand.

They continued practicing and improving, and after several weeks, they performed a recital together for the other patients at the nursing home. Cooperating together, they were able to produce intricate, beautiful music. A gift they thought they had lost forever, the gift of music, was returned to them through the miracle of cooperation. Before Margaret and Ruth learned to play music together, their time in the nursing home had seemed like a prison sentence. Music gave them the joy of living once more.[5]

Musical harmony is often a matter of cooperation. And cooperation is a result of emotional, relational, and spiritual harmony. As we in the church work harmoniously together, we create beautiful music for all the world to hear.

Principle 3: Confirmation

Nehemiah was not merely a boss. He was a genuine leader. When he walked around the perimeter of the city, inspecting the rebuilding of the walls, he didn't see a faceless mass of people. He saw Eliashib and the other temple priests, working hard on rebuilding the Sheep Gate. He saw the sons of Hassenaah setting new doors into the Fish Gate. He greeted Meshullam the son of Berechiah by name and asked him how the work was going and how his family was doing. He took a few moments to chat with Joiada and another Meshullam and tell them what a great job they were doing on the Gate of Yeshanah. He paused to thank Melatiah for bringing his family down from Gibeon to pitch in.

He knew the people who worked on the project—and he knew them all by name. We know that because he lists them in this passage. Nehemiah saw himself as an encourager, a motivator, a cheerleader. He walked around the city walls, affirming the people and confirming their work. A so-called leader who has not learned to encourage, affirm, and confirm the people in an organization is not a true leader at all. That person is just a boss.

This principle holds true whether you are a political leader, a corporate leader, a church leader, or the leader in your family. If you are a mom or a dad, you are a leader. God has called you to encourage, affirm, and confirm the other people in your family, including your spouse and your children. But please understand, this doesn't mean God wants you to heap empty praise on them.

All too often parents and teachers have engaged in a well-intentioned but misguided effort to build the self-esteem of children by withholding needed correction or by lavishing empty praise on them. Psychologist Ann Dunnewold observes that some parents and teachers go to absurd lengths to avoid exposing the little darlings to any experience of upset or adversity. Some teachers, she says, are trained to believe "the child is always right," and if the child ever gives the wrong answer, the teacher should respond, "That is the right answer to another question." Some parents think it's cute to dress their children in a T-shirt that reads, "My parents have never told me no." Dr. Dunnewold concludes:

> We pour on the praise. Every child gets a trophy. Every drawing deserves framing. With my preschool daughter, we well-meaning parents piled on the praise. One day she was drawing as her dad worked nearby. She handed him a page; he exclaimed, "Good job." She whipped out a few more. Dad offered an enthusiastic compliment for each one. She got faster, drawing a single line on several pages and presenting it to him for praise before he caught on. Too much empty praise had led not to creativity but to meaningless repetition for praise's sake... Rather than psychologically sturdy individuals, this approach creates narcissists.[6]

Yes, we need to affirm our children. We need to commend and praise them. We need to build their confidence. But we must not do so with meaningless praise. I encourage you to avoid focusing only on accomplishments and results when you praise your children. This often leads to children feeling that they only have worth when they get all As on their report cards or win the first-place trophy. It's fine to celebrate their triumphs, but don't ever make them feel they've let you down or disappointed you when they have trouble with math or come home with a third-place ribbon.

To affirm and confirm means that you recognize godly traits, Christlike behavior, spiritual growth, and authentic character. Catch your children in the act of being kind, generous, courageous, persistent, industrious, and bold in their witness for Jesus. Affirm their unsuccessful yet courageous attempts as well as their achievements. Tell them you love them and you're proud of them— no matter what.

I think it's significant that Nehemiah doesn't tell us anything about his own job description. He names many people in this chapter and tells us what they did. Their names and their deeds have been recorded in Scripture and read by millions of people for centuries. What greater affirmation could anyone ask?

It's important to understand that Nehemiah didn't simply stand and watch others do all the work. He had his share of sore muscles from lifting stones into place. He probably got calluses from wielding the hammer and chisel. Later, Nehemiah says, "I also persevered in the work on this wall, and we acquired no land, and all my servants were gathered there for the work" (5:16). So both Nehemiah and his assistants took part in the manual labor of building the wall. He may well have had his own section of the wall to rebuild. And as he walked around and inspected the work, he stopped and lent a hand whenever and wherever it was needed. But he reserved the honors, the credit, and the pats on the back for others.

God's Word tells us to give honor to whom honor is owed (see Romans 13:7). Nehemiah was a selfless leader who was eager to give all the honor and credit to others.

Called by God to rebuild our world

It must have been an amazing experience to be used by God to rebuild the holy city of David after all those years of desolation. Yet, it is no less amazing that the Creator of the universe wants to use you and me to rebuild desolate lives, to rebuild the broken walls of the church, to rebuild the broken belief system and value system of our culture. It should amaze us and humble us that God would give us the privilege of using us as his instruments in achieving his eternal plan.

You may have said at one time or another, "I'm only one person. I can't do everything." I confess that I've said words like those all too many times. And when I do, the Lord rebukes me and says, "I ask you to do only what you can do, and to do it by the power of the Holy Spirit. I never call you to do anything without supplying the power to accomplish it."

So each of us must do what we can do to be witnesses for Christ, rebuilding the secure and stable walls of truth in our broken and deceived society. If we are lazy, reluctant, or disobedient, the consequences can be tragic.

Leon Trotsky was one of the leading figures in the Bolshevik Revolution and the founding of the Soviet Union. He was the first leader of the Soviet Red Army and one of the first members of the Politburo. Two years before the Bolshevik Revolution, Trotsky was an exile from Russia living in the United States. A friend invited him to attend a Sunday school class at a church in Chicago. When Trotsky and his friend arrived at the room, they waited—but the Sunday school teacher never showed up. He had not even bothered to have a substitute teacher stand in for him.

Trotsky was offended by the no-show teacher. And for all anyone knows, that may have been his one and only chance to hear the message of God's love and salvation through Jesus Christ. There is no indication that Trotsky ever attended a Sunday school or church again. If that teacher had been present, if he had shared the love of Christ with the young revolutionary, might it have made a difference in history? No one knows. But at the very least, it might have made an eternal difference in the life of Leon Trotsky.

God has called each of us to make a difference in this world. He has commissioned each of us as builders, with a mission to rebuild the broken walls of our society. The church, the body of Christ, needs everybody. Nobody is expendable.

We must stand together as faithful believers, leaving no gap between us. We must consolidate ourselves as one, united behind God's vision. We must cooperate together in achieving God's plan. We must confirm one another and encourage one another in the knowledge that God can do great things in us, through us, and among us.

The Lord called Nehemiah and gave him a plan for rebuilding Jerusalem. Nehemiah consolidated the people, taught them to cooperate, and confirmed them day by day until the mission was accomplished. Now God calls you and me to make a difference in our time, just as Nehemiah did in his. God is calling you by name. What will your answer be?

4

A Spirit of Discouragement

r. John Stapp was a US Air Force colonel and flight surgeon who conducted research on the effects of rapid acceleration and deceleration g-forces on the human body. In the late 1940s, he led research project MX981 at Muroc Army Air Field (now Edwards Air Force Base) in California. The tests involved placing a chimpanzee on a rocket sled, accelerating the sled quickly, then braking it suddenly and measuring the forces experienced by the chimp.

One of Colonel Stapp's assistants was Captain Murphy, who designed the sensors that measured the g-forces. Captain Murphy had one of his assistants install the sensors on the chimpanzee's safety harness. Then the research team strapped the chimp onto the rocket sled and they fired the sled down the test track. The team expected to find that the sensors had registered at least ten g's (or ten times the pull of earth's gravity), but instead the sensors all registered zero.

Clearly, something had gone wrong. After checking the sensors, Captain Murphy discovered that his assistant had wired the sensors incorrectly. Other members of the project MX981 research team blamed Captain Murphy, saying that his diagram of the sensors' wiring was confusing and that he should have double-checked the work of his assistant. But Captain Murphy blamed the underling, saying, "If that guy has any way of making a mistake, he will."

Captain Murphy's saying was eventually condensed to a simple maxim: "If anything can go wrong, it will go wrong." You undoubtedly know that famous maxim as Murphy's Law, though you may not have realized before that there was a real Captain Murphy behind Murphy's Law.[7]

You have probably seen Murphy's Law at work in your own life many times. If you allow the slightest possibility that your plans will go awry, amiss, or amok, they will. But you may not have realized that Murphy's Law works overtime in the spiritual realm. In fact, Murphy's Law is three times as powerful in the spiritual life as it is in the everyday world. Why? Because in the spiritual realm, we constantly have *three* powerful enemies conspiring against us, tripling the possibility that something will go wrong.

Those three enemies of our souls are "the world, the flesh, and the devil." Jesus symbolically referred to these three enemies in the parable of the sower (see Matthew 13:1-8), and Paul, in Ephesians 2:1-3, warns against "following the course of this world," "following the prince of the power of the air" (the devil), and following "the passions of our flesh." Because these three enemies are always conspiring against us, there is a multiplied possibility of spiritual defeat if we allow any of these enemies the slightest toehold in our spiritual lives.

As we examine Nehemiah 4, we see one of these enemies, the

devil, working overtime to defeat Nehemiah, the Jewish people, and the rebuilding project in Jerusalem. Satan is determined to destroy the good work that Nehemiah is doing.

Jesus the builder, Satan the destroyer

Take it from Scripture: If you build, someone will battle you. Where there are friends, there will also be foes. Where there is progress, there will also be obstruction. And in the spiritual realm, whenever you dare great things for God, the devil will try to stop you and punish you. Evangelist D.L. Moody used to say, "The devil never kicks a dead horse." So, if you feel the devil kicking you, rejoice! He only battles those who are making progress for God.

Anytime you begin to gain victory over sin, whenever you begin to triumph over addiction, whenever you begin to achieve consistency in your prayer life, whenever you boldly share your faith with the people around you, don't be surprised at the spiritual opposition that comes your way. The devil's goal is to prevent God's people from attempting great things for God and to keep them from growing in the Christian life.

Two methods Satan frequently uses against us are discouragement and distraction. He employs them together like a one-two punch, hitting us so hard, so fast, so frequently that we are left disoriented by the attack. We see this principle in the opening verses of Nehemiah 4:

> Now when Sanballat heard that we were building the wall, he was angry and greatly enraged, and he jeered at the Jews. And he said in the presence of his brothers and of the army of Samaria, "What are these feeble Jews doing? Will they restore it for themselves? Will they sacrifice? Will they finish up in a day? Will they revive the stones out of

the heaps of rubbish, and burned ones at that?" Tobiah the Ammonite was beside him, and he said, "Yes, what they are building—if a fox goes up on it he will break down their stone wall!" (4:1-3).

We knew that Sanballat the Horonite would be trouble when we first met him in Nehemiah 2. Sanballat was a Samaritan from the town of Horon, who served as a local official of the Persian Empire. When he heard about Nehemiah's building program, he became enraged. He not only hated the Jewish people, but he wanted the land of Samaria, not the land of Judah, to have political and economic preeminence in that region. So he viewed the rebuilding of Jerusalem as a threat to his power and his people. Sanballat, along with Tobiah the Ammonite, jeered and mocked the Jewish people and their rebuilding project.

The devil loves to insult God's work, God's Word, and God's people. Many Christians, unfortunately, can be easily intimidated by insults and mocking words. Some, fearing that they will be rejected and hated by the world, try to alter the words of Scripture and soften the gospel to make it more appealing and less offensive to the world.

In 2011, *Time* magazine named Michigan pastor and author Rob Bell one of the "100 Most Influential People in the World." In his books *Love Wins* and *What We Talk About When We Talk About God,* Bell has challenged a number of major biblical doctrines, including: (1) the claim of the Lord Jesus that he alone is the way, the truth, and the life and the only way to God the Father (see John 14:6); (2) the reality of a literal, eternal hell; and (3) the condemnation of homosexual behavior as sin. Bell claims that the "cultural consciousness has shifted, and this is how the world is," so the church needs to shift toward—and compromise with—the culture.[8]

The problem Bell has is that the Bible clearly says a number of things that he wishes it didn't say. It offends the worldly culture around us when we say that Jesus is the only way to God, that hell is a literal and eternal reality, and that homosexual behavior and homosexual unions are unacceptable to God. Even though God loves homosexual people, just as he loves all sinners, God hates sin. Bell does no one any favors by watering down the truth of God's Word to make it more acceptable to the ever-shifting "cultural consciousness."

Why would a Christian pastor seek to appease cultural consciousness at the expense of biblical truth? Bell seems to think that by erasing the distinctions between the church and the culture, he can make the church more acceptable to the culture. By making the church more like the world, he believes he can persuade the Sanballats of the world to stop mocking and ridiculing and rejecting the church. The problem is that when you erase the distinctions between the world and the church, you erase everything that makes the church distinctly the church.

If you refuse to compromise the Scriptures, you will be mocked and ridiculed. Whenever you take a consistent stand for righteousness and the gospel of Jesus Christ, you can expect derision and persecution. You will be called a "Jesus freak" and a "fanatic." Friends will turn against you. You'll discover enemies you never knew you had.

The student who takes a stand for biblical truth on campus will need the courage of Nehemiah because the professor and most of the other students will be Sanballat. The Christian who talks about his or her faith on social media such as Twitter and Facebook should be prepared for an onslaught of ridicule and mockery because the Internet is heavily populated with worldly, atheistic Sanballats. The Christian journalist or director or entertainer who works in the secular media will have to make almost daily decisions about whether to stand firm for Jesus Christ—or appease and compromise with Sanballat.

And never forget that when you're attacked by the Sanballats of this world, your fight is not actually with them. You are in hand-to-hand combat with Satan. As the apostle Paul told us, "For we do not wrestle against flesh and blood, but against the rulers, against the authorities, against the cosmic powers over this present darkness, against the spiritual forces of evil in the heavenly places" (Ephesians 6:12).

Jesus is the builder; Satan is the destroyer. Jesus is the redeemer; Satan is the corrupter. Jesus is the encourager; Satan is the demoralizer. Satan is always a mocker, a destroyer, and an obstructor. He will always try to tell us that it's impossible for us to rebuild our lives, our marriages, our churches, and our society.

Anytime we attempt great things for God, Sanballat will be there, doing everything possible to demoralize us. And behind Sanballat stands Satan himself.

The prayer of Nehemiah

What did Nehemiah do in the face of opposition from Sanballat? He prayed to God for protection and vindication:

> Hear, O our God, for we are despised. Turn back their taunt on their own heads and give them up to be plundered in a land where they are captives. Do not cover their guilt, and let not their sin be blotted out from your sight, for they have provoked you to anger in the presence of the builders.
>
> So we built the wall. And all the wall was joined together to half its height, for the people had a mind to work.

But when Sanballat and Tobiah and the Arabs and the Ammonites and the Ashdodites heard that the repairing of the walls of Jerusalem was going forward and that the breaches were beginning to be closed, they were very angry. And they all plotted together to come and fight against Jerusalem and to cause confusion in it. And we prayed to our God and set a guard as a protection against them day and night (4:4-9).

Nehemiah's prayer was essentially this: "Lord, our enemies hate us and mistreat us because we serve you and obey you. They may be mocking us, but they're really attacking you through us. Lord, vindicate us. Turn their ridicule back against them and punish them for their sin."

After praying that prayer, Nehemiah went right back to work building the wall—and the wall quickly rose to half its planned height because, as Nehemiah observed, "the people had a mind to work." And when Sanballat, Tobiah, and the rest of their enemies saw that they had failed to stop the work on the walls, they became frustrated and angry. They conspired together and plotted against the reconstruction of Jerusalem.

Again, Nehemiah and the Jewish people responded with a combination of prayer and action. "And we prayed to our God," Nehemiah writes, "and set a guard as a protection against them day and night."

When your enemies sneer at you for doing God's work, don't be discouraged. Don't be intimidated. Don't be deterred. Take a moment to pray—then keep moving forward, keep doing the work God has given you to do. Prayer is your first obligation, not your last resort.

And as you pray, be watchful. Nehemiah not only asked God for protection, but he set a guard to protect the work day and night. Here we see the perfect balance of spirituality and practicality. Nehemiah remained spiritually alert in prayer—and he and his people remained physically watchful all around the city walls.

We will soon see the wisdom of this two-pronged strategy of praying and watching, because the opposition from Sanballat and his coconspirators is about to intensify.

The weapon of discouragement

Not only did Satan thrust opposition in their way, but he also tempted the Jewish people to become discouraged, fearful, and demoralized. Nehemiah records:

> In Judah it was said, "The strength of those who bear the burdens is failing. There is too much rubble. By ourselves we will not be able to rebuild the wall." And our enemies said, "They will not know or see till we come among them and kill them and stop the work." At that time the Jews who lived near them came from all directions and said to us ten times, "You must return to us." So in the lowest parts of the space behind the wall, in open places, I stationed the people by their clans, with their swords, their spears, and their bows. And I looked and arose and said to the nobles and to the officials and to the rest of the people, "Do not be afraid of them. Remember the Lord, who is great and awesome, and fight for your brothers, your sons, your daughters, your wives, and your homes" (4:10-14).

Discouragement is the chief occupational hazard of being a Christian. Discouragement is the devil's best weapon against us. If Satan auctioned off his entire arsenal of weapons, the weapon known as discouragement would be sold for the highest bid. This feeling we call discouragement comes in many shapes and varieties, ranging from merely feeling the blahs or the blues all the way to clinical depression. Discouragement can attack you even when you are walking faithfully with God.

One reason discouragement is such an effective weapon against the believer is that Satan can often inflict it on us just as we are experiencing a spiritual high, a mountaintop experience with God. In 1 Kings 18, the prophet Elijah singlehandedly defeated the prophets of Baal, profoundly altering the political and spiritual structure of Israel. It was an amazing victory, and Elijah experienced joy beyond measure. But in the very next chapter, Elijah fled for his life from Jezebel, and he went out into the wilderness and sat under a broom tree, praying to God that he might die: "It is enough; now, O Lord, take away my life" (1 Kings 19:4).

The prophet Jonah preached a message of repentance in the ancient Assyrian city of Nineveh, and the people responded beyond all expectations. Thousands of people turned to God to be saved. Jonah should have been thrilled. Yet in Jonah 4, we find the prophet sitting dejectedly in the wilderness, and he is actually angry with God because of the success of his mission! "O Lord," he prays bitterly, "please take my life from me, for it is better for me to die than to live" (Jonah 4:3).

If you surrender to the spirit of discouragement, you rob yourself of hope. You surrender to Satan's will for your life. Many Christians face discouragement today, saying, "I quit. I can't go on. I won't go on." I urge you: do not surrender to discouragement. Take a lesson from the story of Nehemiah and the people of Jerusalem. They were tempted to give in to discouragement, but they made a choice to persevere with God—and God gave them the encouragement they needed, the encouragement to continue working and building.

And God wants to encourage you as well. No matter what you are going through, no matter how dejected and demoralized you feel right now, God is ready to encourage you as he encouraged the people of Israel. I'm not suggesting that you should simply put on a happy face. You can't ignore your discouragement any more than you can ignore the gas gauge in your car. If you are running on empty, and you keep pressing the accelerator, you are going to run out of gas.

But God does not say to us, "Even though your tank is empty, just pretend it's full." He wants to fill your spiritual tank with encouragement—realistic, dynamic, powerful encouragement. That's what God did for Nehemiah and his people, and that is what God wants to do for you. Let's look at Nehemiah's example and see how he dealt with the problem of discouragement.

First, Nehemiah realized that the people had reached a point of physical exhaustion. He writes, "In Judah it was said, 'The strength of those who bear the burdens is failing. There is too much rubble. By ourselves we will not be able to rebuild the wall.'" The people had worked so hard that they were dead tired and emotionally depleted. Not only was the work physically demanding, but they faced the constant stress of the threats and ridicule of their enemies. No wonder the people were prime candidates for discouragement.

Are you facing pressure and stress in your job? Are you facing exhaustion and stress in your home? When you are physically tired and emotionally spent, watch out. You are a candidate for discouragement.

Second, Nehemiah realized that the people had lost sight of their goal. They had taken their eyes off the vision of a restored Jerusalem, and all they could see was the rubble that surrounded them. Worse yet, all they could think of was the Herculean task of clearing away all of that rubble. One of the most important tasks of leadership is to give the people a vision of a brighter future. If the people don't have a vision to aim for, they quickly become vulnerable to discouragement.

The complaints of discouragement came from the tribe of Judah, which was no average tribe. This was the leading tribe, the strongest tribe in the nation of Israel, yet they had become discouraged and disheartened. It was one thing for Israel's external enemies—Sanballat, Tobiah, and Geshem—to inflict discouragement on the people. That's what you expect enemies to do. But when your own leadership begins to surrender to discouragement, your nation is in double trouble.

What do you do when the people you count on, the people you look up to for leadership, turn weak at the knees? What do you do when your heroes begin to faint from discouragement?

The people had reached the halfway point of the building program—and they had worked mightily. A few verses earlier, Nehemiah had said, "And all the wall was joined together to half its height, for the people had a mind to work." But the halfway point is often a dangerous place for any project, any building program, any major undertaking. That's the very point where discouragement sets in. The people look back upon all they have accomplished, and then they look ahead and see how far they still have to go and how much rubble remains to be cleared away—and their hearts sink.

Many people feel this way at the midpoint of their lives. That is why they often experience what we call "a midlife crisis." They say, "Look at my background. Look at my past failures. Look at all my broken dreams lying in the dust. Look at all the things I hoped to accomplish and never will. Look at all the debris of mistakes, regrets, and abandoned dreams cluttering my life. I can't go on. I wish I could die."

If that is how you feel today, listen to the voice of God. He is saying to you, "Trust me, turn to me, I can clear away the debris of your life." You may find it hard to hear his voice right now. Perhaps the sound of God's voice is muffled because you are listening to the noise of discouragement.

God speaks softly. He won't shout at us. We need to quiet our hearts and shut out the noise of discouragement. We need to listen for his encouragement.

As the people battled discouragement within, they also faced an external threat. Fear is contagious, and Nehemiah knew he had to put some steel in the spines of his people and prepare them for the fight ahead. Their enemies were saying of the Jewish people, "They will not know or see till we come among them and kill them and stop the work."

A fascinating little detail is tucked away in this passage and easy to miss, yet it is extremely important for our lives today. Nehemiah tells us, "At that time the Jews who lived near [the enemies] came from all directions and said to us ten times, 'You must return to us.'" Who were the most fearful Jews in that land? The ones who lived nearest the enemy! Nehemiah says that they came and begged him ten times to come to them because they were so terrified of the enemy.

What was true in Nehemiah's day is still true today: When you live too close to your enemy, you will be a bundle of nerves. So don't get cozy with the enemy. Don't compromise with sin. When you live close to Satan, when you let him have a toehold of sin in your life, you will experience inordinate fear. That's what always comes from living too close to the enemy.

In 2 Timothy 1:7, Paul tells us, "For God gave us a spirit not of fear but of power and love and self-control." Are you living in fear? If so, you know that your fear does not come from God. Are you living in close proximity to the devil? Have you given Satan a window of opportunity in your life? Who do you listen to? Who do you talk to? Are you listening to the encouragement of the Lord—or the threats and discouraging words of your enemy?

Nehemiah responded quickly to the fears of his people. He stationed his people, clan by clan, along the wall and armed them for battle. The people kept their swords, spears, and bows close to their work implements. Then Nehemiah stood before the people and said, "Do not be afraid of them. Remember the Lord, who is great and awesome, and fight for your brothers, your sons, your daughters, your wives, and your homes."

The encouragement of fellow believers

In Nehemiah 3, we saw Nehemiah playing the role of a cheerleader, going around the perimeter of the city, greeting people by name, commending them on the good work they were doing. Here in Nehemiah 4, we see him playing the role of a coach during a big game—and he is calling, "Time out!" He is calling his team off the field and into the huddle for a pep talk and strategy session.

Many a football game has been lost in the last minutes or seconds because the coach failed to use his timeouts in a strategic way. But Coach Nehemiah has the winning game plan. He reminds his players to stick to the fundamentals—faith in our great and awesome God. He reminds them of what they're playing for—their brothers, sons, daughters, wives, and homes. And he reminds them not to be afraid but to take the battle straight to the opponent.

Let me suggest to you a reading assignment for times of discouragement. Read Isaiah 53 at least once a week, and read it whenever you feel discouraged. This Old Testament passage reveals to us the suffering and heartache of our Savior, our Messiah, Jesus the Lord. In that passage we read:

> He was despised and rejected by men;
>   a man of sorrows, and acquainted with grief;
> and as one from whom men hide their faces
>   he was despised, and we esteemed him not.
> Surely he has borne our griefs
>   and carried our sorrows;
> yet we esteemed him stricken,
>   smitten by God, and afflicted.
> But he was pierced for our transgressions;
>   he was crushed for our iniquities;
> upon him was the chastisement that brought us peace,
>   and with his wounds we are healed.
>   (Isaiah 53:3-5)

The Lord knows your discouragement. He knows your fears. And he has the cure for discouragement and fear: "Remember the Lord, who is great and awesome." Instead of looking at the rubble around you and listening to the threats of your enemies, lift your eyes to the Lord and listen to his words of encouragement and reassurance.

Remember too how Nehemiah grouped the people around the walls in families, in clans. There is a reason why Nehemiah did that. We find safety and encouragement when we join together with other godly people. We find security in meeting together with other members of our family of faith, our fellow believers, the people in our church family who love us and care for us. That's why it's important to not merely attend church on Sundays but to also be involved in a small group Bible study—a place of close fellowship and friendship where we can be free to be ourselves. In a small group fellowship, we can confess our fears, failures, and sins, and experience the freedom of forgiveness. We all need the fellowship of other believers who will care for us and pray for us throughout the week, as we care and pray for them.

I've heard it said that a friend is someone who comes in when the rest of the world goes out. I feel grateful that I have such friends in my life. Do you have friends like that in your life today? If not, it's time to start being a friend to other believers and to start drawing those believers into your life.

Ready to build—and ready for battle

Next, Nehemiah describes the state of perpetual vigilance and readiness that the people maintained as they completed the construction of the wall:

> When our enemies heard that it was known to us and that God had frustrated their plan, we all returned to the wall, each to his work. From that day on, half of my servants worked on construction, and half held the spears, shields, bows, and coats of mail. And the leaders stood behind the whole house of Judah, who were building on the wall. Those who carried burdens were loaded in such a way that each labored on the work with one hand and held his weapon with the other. And each of the builders had his sword strapped at his side while he built. The man who sounded the trumpet was beside me. And I said

to the nobles and to the officials and to the rest of the people, "The work is great and widely spread, and we are separated on the wall, far from one another. In the place where you hear the sound of the trumpet, rally to us there. Our God will fight for us."

So we labored at the work, and half of them held the spears from the break of dawn until the stars came out. I also said to the people at that time, "Let every man and his servant pass the night within Jerusalem, that they may be a guard for us by night and may labor by day." So neither I nor my brothers nor my servants nor the men of the guard who followed me, none of us took off our clothes; each kept his weapon at his right hand (4:15-23).

The people of Israel found themselves rebuilding the city and fighting their enemies at the same time. They carried a trowel in one hand and a sword in the other.

Some in the church today only want to build the church. They don't like to engage in battle. They don't want to engage in spiritual warfare. They don't want to battle the Sanballat of secularism, the Tobiah of immorality, and the Geshem of false religion. They just want to build the church and ignore the battle raging all around them.

But Nehemiah wants us to know that each of us is called both to build and to do battle. We are to wield both the trowel and the sword. We do not have the option of being noncombatants in the spiritual warfare going on around us. Our enemy, the devil, has not left that option open to us. If we do not fight, we will be casualties.

A few years ago, one of the most dominant players in the National Football League was Reggie White, the man they called "the Minister of Defense." He earned that title because he was a committed minister of the gospel of Jesus Christ as well as a defensive end for the Philadelphia Eagles and the Green Bay Packers. Though he died at age forty-three of a lung ailment in 2004, he is still remembered as one of the legendary players of the game.

During one game when Reggie played for the Eagles, he was rushing through the offensive line on play after play. The unfortunate offensive lineman who was assigned to block Reggie could hardly slow him down. On one play, Reggie ran right over his opponent, leaving the man flat on his back. After the play was over, Reggie put out his hand to help the man up. "Jesus loves you," Reggie said, "and I love you too—but man, you'd better learn how to block."

The same is true for you and me as God's people. It's not enough to know how to build. We'd better learn how to block. We'd better learn to defend what God has enabled us to build. We better learn how to block for our families. We better learn how to block for our faith. We better learn how to block for the church.

As Christians, we must constantly guard against those who would destroy what God has built. We need to be thrice-vigilant in guarding our souls because we face a triple enemy—the world, the flesh, and the devil. And there is a moral and spiritual Murphy's Law that says that if we permit an opening for anything to go wrong in our spiritual lives, it *will* go wrong. So we must not give our enemy an opening to defeat us.

Nehemiah coached his players in how to block the enemy. He taught them how to watch and pray. He encouraged them, motivated them, and lifted their spirits by lifting their eyes toward God. As Nehemiah said to the people, "The work is great and widely spread, and we are separated on the wall, far from one another. In the place where you hear the sound of the trumpet, rally to us there. Our God will fight for us."

For us as believers in the twenty-first century, the task we face is still great. We are tempted to succumb to discouragement. But we serve a great and awesome God. When we hear the sound of the trumpet, we will rally together, we will encourage one another, we will pray and care for one another, and our God will fight for us.

5

Freedom from Financial Bondage

D arius I (550–486 BC) was one of the great kings of Persia
and the grandfather of the Persian king Artaxerxes, who is
described in the book of Nehemiah. He conquered the Babylonian Empire in approximately 516 BC. When Darius arrived in
Babylon to be received as the conquered nation's new king, he saw
the tomb of the Queen Nitocris, whose husband, Nebuchadnezzar, had conquered Jerusalem. The queen's tomb bore the inscription, "If any king of Babylon after me should be in need of money,
he may open this tomb and take as much as he wants, but only if
he is truly in need."

Though Darius was rich beyond measure, it troubled him that
such a vast hoard of riches lay unused in the woman's tomb. So he
ordered the tomb to be opened, and he went inside to see the treasure with his own eyes—but the tomb was bare. Nothing lay there
but the embalmed body of the queen and a message: "If you had

not been greedy for gold, you would not have thought of ransacking the graves of the departed."

Greed is a serious moral defect in a leader. In Nehemiah 5, we will see that a leader's moral character is extremely important to his effectiveness. A great leader seeks God's blessing for the people he leads and is not concerned with personal gain. One of the most reliable indicators of the character of a leader is the way that leader responds to the temptation of greed.

Money is one of the most popular and pervasive subjects in our popular media today. The subject of money usually gets our attention—unless the subject is brought up in church. Few of us like to hear sermons preached about money, and we don't like to read Christian books about money. We like to hear about ways to make money and ways to spend money, but we don't like to hear about our financial responsibility toward God. We don't like to hear that we will be held accountable by God for the way we have handled our money.

As I write these words, I am keenly aware that you may not want to hear what I have to say. But I have a duty to write these words, because the fifth chapter of Nehemiah is all about money and the moral and spiritual responsibility that money imposes on us. Equally important, this chapter deals with a particular aspect of money that is timely for us today.

Who is your master?

The French Enlightenment writer and philosopher Voltaire once observed in a letter to a friend, "When it is a question of money, everybody is of the same religion." I'm not sure what he meant by that, but one possible interpretation is that we all tend to make money our god instead of making God our God. If that is what Voltaire meant, then he was expressing much the same sentiment we find in Job 12. There, Job says that evil people who provoke God with their sin "bring their god in their hand"—and the god they hold in their hand is their money (see Job 12:6).

In *Atlas Shrugged*, novelist Ayn Rand relates a conversation between two men.

"You know," says one, "money is the root of all evil."

"So you think that money is the root of all evil?" the other man replies. "Money is made possible only by the men who produce. Is this what you consider evil?"[9]

You are probably already aware of that "money is the root of all evil" is a badly misquoted version of the apostle Paul's counsel to Timothy: "For *the love of money* is a root of all kinds of evils. It is through this craving that some have wandered away from the faith and pierced themselves with many pangs" (1 Timothy 6:10).

Clearly, money itself is not an evil thing, nor is it the root of all evil in the world. But the *love* of money—the greedy impulse to accumulate money and especially the desire to "get rich quick" by acquiring what we have not earned—is in fact at the root of all kinds of evils and sins in the world.

Money itself is a morally neutral commodity, and we can use money for a variety of good and noble purposes. Money puts a roof over our heads and food on the table. Money prints Bibles and powers Christian radio stations. Money sends the gospel of Jesus Christ to every distant corner of the globe. As Ayn Rand observed, money is made possible by people who are productive, who work hard, and who add value to the economy. So let's be careful not to misinterpret what the Bible says about money. This medium of exchange is morally and spiritually neutral, and it can be put to both good uses and evil uses. It is the *love* of money that produces all kinds of evil in the world.

One of the surest ways of measuring a person's character is to observe how that person handles wealth and material possessions. Sanctimonious talk and religious words do not reveal the reality of a person's character or soul. But a glance at that person's bank statement speaks volumes.

When historian Godfrey Davies was researching *Wellington and His Army*, a 1954 biography of the Duke of Wellington, he said, "I found an old account ledger that showed how the Duke spent his money. It was a far better clue to what he thought was really important than the reading of his letters or speeches."[10] What would your spending habits say about your deepest beliefs, your values, and your character? Does your spending align with what you say you believe—or does your spending contradict your words?

God knows us well. He knows that the way we use money is a window into our souls. That's why there are two thousand verses in God's Word that speak directly to our handling of our money and our possessions. Moreover, the Lord Jesus spoke more about the right and wrong use of money and possessions than he said about heaven and hell combined. Why does God have so much to say in his Word about money and possessions? It's because our attitude and behavior toward money is directly related to our spiritual condition.

In the Sermon on the Mount, Jesus said, "No one can serve two masters, for either he will hate the one and love the other, or he will be devoted to the one and despise the other. You cannot serve God and money" (Matthew 6:24). Either God is your Master or money is your master. If you serve one, you'll have no time left over to serve the other. A servant of money cannot be a servant of Jesus. And if you are not a servant of Jesus, you cannot spend eternity with Jesus.

That's why Jesus also said in that very same sermon, "Do not lay up for yourselves treasures on earth, where moth and rust destroy and where thieves break in and steal, but lay up for yourselves treasures in heaven, where neither moth nor rust destroys and where thieves do not break in and steal. For where your treasure is, there your heart will be also" (Matthew 6:19-21). How do you lay up treasures in heaven? By giving your earthly treasures away to the work of God's kingdom.

God has entrusted many material blessings to you and me. We will either handle those blessings as faithful stewards and servants of God or we will mishandle them, to our lasting regret. We are either the master of our money and material possessions or we will be mastered by them. Money is a useful servant but a terrible master.

A society-wide crisis of debt

In Nehemiah 5 we see one of the worst examples of the misuse of money in all of Scripture:

Now there arose a great outcry of the people and of their wives against their Jewish brothers. For there were those who said, "With our sons and our daughters, we are many. So let us get grain, that we may eat and keep alive." There were also those who said, "We are mortgaging our fields, our vineyards, and our houses to get grain because of the famine." And there were those who said, "We have borrowed money for the king's tax on our fields and our vineyards. Now our flesh is as the flesh of our brothers, our children are as their children. Yet we are forcing our sons and our daughters to be slaves, and some of our daughters have already been enslaved, but it is not in our power to help it, for other men have our fields and our vineyards" (5:1-5).

The people of Nehemiah's time had become enslaved by money. They were in financial bondage. Even their sons and daughters were forced into literal slavery because of their financial bondage. As a result, there was great division, anger, and outcry among the people.

Understand, the wall is still only half-finished—and half a wall is not much better than no wall at all. The city of Jerusalem is still insecure and wide-open to its enemies. Yet the people who are rebuilding the wall, who were once consolidated and unified and working together as one, have now become divided. The rebuilding project has been thrown into crisis because of the wrongful use of money.

Satan often uses money as a wedge to divide Christians from each other, to divide husband from wife, parents from children, one business partner from another, one church member from another, and one citizen from another.

Nehemiah goes on to tell us that the misuse and abuse of money had led to shortages of the necessities of life, accompanied by price gouging: "For there were those who said, 'With our sons and our daughters, we are many. So let us get grain, that we may eat and keep alive.'" Some of the Israelites were mortgaged up to their eyeballs: "There were also those who said, 'We are mortgaging our fields, our vineyards, and our houses to get grain because of the famine.'"

Does this situation sound familiar to you? The people were drowning in debt. They were borrowing money just to survive—and even borrowing to pay their taxes: "And there were those who said, 'We have borrowed money for the king's tax on our fields and our vineyards.'" The Bible teaches clearly that we are not to overextend ourselves through borrowing and accumulating debt. The Bible does not prohibit us from borrowing per se, but it does teach that we are to repay our debts quickly so as not to become slaves to debt.

God's Word teaches that instead of being debtors, we should be givers. The psalmist wrote: "The wicked borrows but does not pay back, but the righteous is generous and gives" (Psalm 37:21). Debt steals our ability to live generously toward others. Sometimes financial necessity, such as the loss of a job or a business setback, forces us to go into debt merely to survive. But all too many Christians have used easy credit to fund their greed instead of to meet their need. They have mortgaged their financial freedom in order to acquire a newer car, a boat, an RV, or a big house they can't afford.

Paul warned the first-century Christians to avoid debt. He wrote, "Owe no one anything, except to love each other, for the one who loves another has fulfilled the law" (Romans 13:8). When Paul says, "Owe no one anything," he means *stay out of debt*!

Nehemiah's people were in bondage to debt—a state of complete financial slavery. They had mortgaged the future of their children. They said, "We are forcing our sons and our daughters to be slaves, and some of our daughters have already been enslaved, but it is not in our power to help it, for other men have our fields and our vineyards." And isn't that exactly the situation we find ourselves in all across Western civilization? Isn't that exactly what America has done, piling up a mountain of debt, then leaving it for the next generation to pay?

The people had mortgaged their fields and vineyards and were working night and day to pay off their debts, yet they owed so much that no matter how hard they worked, they continued to fall behind. Even after forcing their own children into slavery, they still had no hope of climbing out of their black hole of debt.

The problem of debt was a society-wide crisis in Nehemiah's day, and the national debt is a society-wide crisis in twenty-first-century America. If you thought America's fiscal crisis was something new in history, then Nehemiah 5 is probably an eye-opener for you. One of the unmistakable signs of a civilization in decline is spiraling public debt—and a corrupt political class that will not bring borrowing and spending under control.

Are you in denial?

God never intended for his people to be in financial bondage. That is not his will for any follower of Christ. So I ask you, are you free in Christ? Or are you living in financial bondage? And while I'm meddling in your personal finances, let me ask you this: Do you give to God the firstfruits of your labor—or the leftovers?

God told Israel, "The best of the firstfruits of your ground you shall bring into the house of the Lord your God" (Exodus 23:19). And God went on to promise Israel:

> "And if you faithfully obey the voice of the Lord your God, being careful to do all his commandments that I command you today, the Lord your God will set you high above all the nations of the earth. And all these blessings shall come upon you and overtake you, if you obey the voice of the Lord your God. Blessed shall you be in the city, and blessed shall you be in the field. Blessed shall be the fruit of your womb and the fruit of your ground and the fruit of your cattle, the increase of your herds and the young of your flock. Blessed shall be your basket and your kneading bowl. Blessed shall you be when you come in, and blessed shall you be when you go out" (Deuteronomy 28:1-6).

And that is just the beginning of the promises God makes to those who faithfully obey his commandments. He promises to bless the land and the barns, the livestock and the ground. He promises to open his heavenly treasury and pour out his blessing upon us. He promises to bless the work of our hands. He promises to make our nation economically strong—if we obey his commandments. And he also promises serious consequences if we disobey.

God makes these promises to us because he wants to bless us. He wants to liberate us and lead us in victory, but Satan wants to deceive us and keep us in bondage. What happens to people when they find themselves in financial bondage? They quickly come into conflict with each other. They become divided, distrustful, and resentful toward each other. We see this principle at work in marriages and business partnerships and churches all around us. And we see this principle at work here in Nehemiah 5. We see the people turning on one another and attacking one another because they are in financial bondage.

As you read these words, you may find yourself feeling irritated, defensive, and perhaps even angry. You may be thinking, *Yes, I have financial pressures in my life, but you don't understand my situation. You have no right to preach at me. My situation is different. I'm not like those people in Nehemiah 5. You have no right to meddle in my financial affairs.*

If those are your thoughts and emotions right now, then I would ask you to consider this next question. Consider it as honestly and searchingly as you can, with full awareness that you may be feeling defensive, and you may even be in denial. The question is this: Could it be that the irritation and anger you feel is a direct result of the financial bondage you're in? Could it be that you are actually angry with yourself because of the unwise financial choices you have made?

If you were experiencing the blessing of financial freedom, you would not be feeling angry. The anger you feel is a direct result of your financial bondage. And remember, Satan's strategy is to divide God's people over the issue of money. If Satan can divide God's people, he can stop the work of God. As we see in Nehemiah 5, Satan tried to divide God's people in order to stop the rebuilding of the walls of Jerusalem.

The devil has always tried to divide and conquer God's people. That is still his strategy today.

Making restitution

There was another group of people in Nehemiah 5 who were misusing and abusing money. Nehemiah addresses this group next:

> I was very angry when I heard their outcry and these words. I took counsel with myself, and I brought charges against the nobles and the officials. I said to them, "You are exacting interest, each from his brother." And I held a great assembly against them and said to them, "We, as far as we are able, have bought back our Jewish brothers who have been sold to the nations, but you even sell your brothers that they may be sold to us!" They were silent and could not find a word to say. So I said, "The thing that you are doing is not good. Ought you not to walk in the fear of our God to prevent the taunts of the nations our enemies? Moreover, I and my brothers and my servants are lending them money and grain. Let us abandon this exacting of interest. Return to them this very day their fields, their vineyards, their olive orchards, and their houses, and the percentage of money, grain, wine, and oil that you have been exacting from them." Then they said, "We will restore these and require nothing from them. We will do as you say." And I called the priests and made them swear to

> do as they had promised. I also shook out the fold of my
> garment and said, "So may God shake out every man
> from his house and from his labor who does not keep this
> promise. So may he be shaken out and emptied." And all
> the assembly said "Amen" and praised the LORD. And the
> people did as they had promised (5:6-13).

The second group Nehemiah had to confront were the nobles and rulers of that society. These people had money, but they used their money for manipulation, exploitation, and gaining power over their neighbors. This passage tells us that the wealthy nobles and rulers charged exorbitant interest rates. Though Nehemiah was angry over the injustice he saw, he responded with self-control. He came up with a creative idea to solve the problem—and both sides accepted his solution.

The debtors repented of going into debt, and the lenders repented of breaking God's laws and placing their Jewish brothers and sisters in bondage. The nobles and rulers had taken advantage of their own people. But now they said, "We will restore these and require nothing from them. We will do as you say." They would return the fields, vineyards, orchards, and houses to the people, and they would refund the silver, gold, grain, wine, and oil they had taken as interest on the debt.

We see this same repentant spirit in the tax collector Zacchaeus when he encountered Jesus and committed his life to the Lord. Zacchaeus said, "Behold, Lord, the half of my goods I give to the poor. And if I have defrauded anyone of anything, I restore it fourfold" (see Luke 19:8). That kind of generosity can come only from a truly repentant heart. If you want God to bless you, but you owe money to someone, make restitution—then see what God accomplishes in your life.

Nehemiah's first money management principle

The next section of Nehemiah 5 teaches us three key money management principles that are as valid today as they were in Nehemiah's day. Nehemiah's first money management principle is: "Put God first." He writes:

> Moreover, from the time that I was appointed to be their governor in the land of Judah, from the twentieth year to the thirty-second year of Artaxerxes the king, twelve years, neither I nor my brothers ate the food allowance of the governor. The former governors who were before me laid heavy burdens on the people and took from them for their daily ration forty shekels of silver. Even their servants lorded it over the people. But I did not do so, because of the fear of God. I also persevered in the work on this wall, and we acquired no land, and all my servants were gathered there for the work (5:14-16).

Nehemiah was appointed by the king to be the governor, yet he refused to take advantage of his position in order to reap a profit for himself, as other governors did. It would have been perfectly legal for Nehemiah to profit from his position, but he set aside his personal rights to put God first.

Why did he forgo his rights? He explains, "because of the fear of God." This doesn't mean Nehemiah was afraid God would punish him. The phrase "the fear of God" is used throughout Scripture to refer to an intense reverence for God and obedience toward God, rooted in an awed appreciation of the infinite greatness, power, and righteousness of God.

Though Nehemiah, as a governor of Babylon, had the legal right to exploit his position under Persian law, he answered to a higher law, a higher Authority. He lived by the ethical principles of the law of God because he had a righteous fear of God.

Though Jesus would not come to earth and preach the Sermon on the Mount until five centuries later, Nehemiah lived by the principle Jesus declared in Matthew 6:33: "But seek first the kingdom of God and his righteousness, and all these things will be added to you." The lordship of God dominated his life and determined his actions. He was ruled by love for God, not the love of money or the accumulation of material possessions. Nehemiah rejected the values of his peers, who were all engaged in laying up treasures on earth. He chose instead to lay up treasures in heaven. Nehemiah chose to put God first.

If money is our god, then we will be enslaved by our god. If God is our God, then we are truly free. Money is an idol that devours its worshipers. Our God is a God who welcomes his worshipers as his children and as friends.

Nehemiah goes on to say, "I also persevered in the work on this wall, and we acquired no land, and all my servants were gathered there for the work." When Nehemiah arrived in Jerusalem, he could have acquired land and could have taken advantage of the needy people, but he refused to do that. He did not come to Jerusalem to make a killing in the real estate market. He came to rebuild the city wall. He and his servants came to work, not to get rich. He chose to be honest, ethical, and godly in all his financial dealings.

Nehemiah put God first, whether he was the cupbearer to the king in Susa or the leader of the construction crew in Jerusalem. He loved God, not money. If you put God first in your life, he will unshackle you and set you free from the love of money.

Nehemiah's second money management principle

Nehemiah's second money management principle is: "It is more blessed to give than to receive." Nehemiah writes:

> Moreover, there were at my table 150 men, Jews and officials, besides those who came to us from the nations that were around us. Now what was prepared at my expense for each day was one ox and six choice sheep and birds, and every ten days all kinds of wine in abundance. Yet for all this I did not demand the food allowance of the governor, because the service was too heavy on this people. Remember for my good, O my God, all that I have done for this people (5:17-19).

Nehemiah hosted a daily banquet at his own expense, and 150 Jewish leaders ate at his table every day. And he didn't serve baked beans out of a can. He served a lavish array of choice foods—ox, sheep, and fowl, along with an abundance of excellent wine. Nehemiah was abundantly generous toward others, and God continually supplied everything he needed. Though Nehemiah could have taxed the people to support these banquets, he depended on God. As God provided, Nehemiah gave—and he became a conduit for blessing.

Nehemiah exemplified the principle Jesus later proclaimed: "Give, and it will be given to you. Good measure, pressed down, shaken together, running over, will be put into your lap. For with the measure you use it will be measured back to you" (Luke 6:38). Or as Jesus also said, "It is more blessed to give than to receive" (see Acts 20:35).

It was almost as if Nehemiah had an addiction to giving—but that's an excellent addiction to have! If you have learned how to give, then you can experience the joy of Christmas, the season of giving, all year round. As Paul writes, "Each one must give as he has decided in his heart, not reluctantly or under compulsion, for God loves a cheerful giver" (2 Corinthians 9:7). The original Greek word translated "cheerful" is *hilaros*, from which we get our English word hilarious.

If you are familiar with Charles Dickens's *A Christmas Carol*, you'll recall that after Ebenezer Scrooge undergoes a radical change of heart, he gives away money and presents to strangers, and then he presents the Cratchit family with a lavish Christmas dinner. Whenever Scrooge gives gifts to people, he laughs hysterically, hilariously, so that people think he must have gone crazy. But Scrooge has not lost his mind—he has come to his senses. He has become a cheerful giver. The reformed Ebenezer Scrooge is a picture of what a cheerful, hilarious giver should look like.

I would love to see hilarity in the congregation as we pass the offering plate. I would love to see laughter break out as Christians come to their senses, lose their inhibitions, and give to the cause of Christ. Some people say, "Give till it hurts." I say, give till it's hilarious. Give till you feel so blessed that you just can't keep from laughing!

You will never be able to give hilariously as long as you think by the world's logic. Hilarious giving is possible only for those who think by heavenly logic. The world says that if you give your money and possessions away, you will be poorer. Jesus says that if you give your money and possessions away, you'll be rich and blessed— "pressed down, shaken together, running over, will be put into your lap."

The world says that your net worth is the sum total of your real estate holdings, your personal assets, and your investments. The logic of heaven says that your net worth is the sum total of all you give away. The Bible never emphasizes what you own. It always emphasizes what you give. Those who love the world seek to conserve their assets and possessions. Those who love Jesus seek to give. Those who love the world are in bondage to their possessions. Those who love Jesus are liberated and cheerfully free to give.

When I think of how people are enslaved by their love of money, I'm reminded of the elephants of Thailand. When a wild elephant is captured in Thailand, he must be tamed and domesticated. So the captor will attach a heavy chain to one of the elephant's legs and anchor it to a massive banyan tree. The elephant will struggle against the chain for days, and finally he will learn that the struggle is useless. He cannot break or dislodge the chain. So the elephant surrenders.

Once the elephant has accepted enslavement, the elephant's handlers can attach a smaller, lighter chain, and anchor it to the ground with a small iron stake. The elephant could easily yank the stake out of the ground and go wherever he wishes, and the elephant handlers could not stop him. But the elephant doesn't know that. Mentally, he is still chained to the banyan tree. He has accepted his slavery.

We surrender to financial bondage in much the same way. Instead of changing our spending behavior and borrowing behavior, we surrender to our chains of debt. We accumulate possessions on credit instead of giving hilariously and cheerfully. We may have a *desire* to give, but we have no *design* to give. We do not consciously and intentionally plan our giving. So we remain chained to one little place, foolishly and needlessly enslaved, because we do not realize we have the power to choose freedom.

I challenge you to think seriously about how to become financially free. You may need to consult with a nonprofit debt counselor, take a course in financial stewardship at your church, or read a book on financial stewardship such as *Financial Peace Revisited* and *The Total Money Makeover* by Dave Ramsey, and *The Treasure Principle* and *Managing God's Money* by Randy Alcorn. The Bible says that on the first day of the week, God's people should set aside the amount of money they have chosen to give. Empowered by God, you can set yourself free from financial bondage. You can plan to give systematically to the Lord's work.

When you exercise systematic giving, you give deliberately and thoughtfully, under the leading of God's Spirit. Without a disciplined way of giving, you end up being dragged from cause to cause by one emotional appeal after another. One well-known televangelist told his TV audience that if they did not donate a total of several million dollars by a certain date, God would "take him home." He would die, and his death would be their fault! This is nothing but emotional blackmail. Emotions are a poor guide to effective Christian giving. Don't be dragged around by your emotions. Follow the wise and gentle leading of the Holy Spirit.

Nehemiah's third money management principle

Nehemiah's third money management principle is: "You can't out give God." Nehemiah depended on God to supply all his needs, and God never let him down. Put God first in your life, and you will be freed from financial bondage—and God will take care of you. You cannot out give God. But you must learn to master your money and not be mastered by it.

God is the giver of all good and perfect gifts. As Jesus himself said, "For God so loved the world, that he gave his only Son, that whoever believes in him should not perish but have eternal life" (John 3:16). And Paul said, "Thanks be to God for his inexpressible gift!" (2 Corinthians 9:15). When Paul considered the gift God had given him, he said, in effect, "I can't explain it, I can't describe it, I can't express it—I can only give thanks for it." The gift of God—the gift of our redemption through the Lord's sacrifice on the cross, the gift of salvation from the eternal hell we richly deserve—is impossible to explain.

If our greatest need had been information, God would have sent us an educator. If our greatest need had been technology, God would have sent us an engineer. If our greatest need had been money, God would have sent us an economist. If our greatest need had been fun, God would have sent us an entertainer. But our greatest need of all was our need for forgiveness, so God sent us a Savior, Jesus Christ, to bring us eternal life.

Do you want to live a Christlike life? Then stop accumulating possessions. Start giving, generously and hilariously. Receive the freedom God brings you.

In 1971, composer and conductor Leonard Bernstein premiered a musical theater piece called *MASS*, commissioned by Jacqueline Kennedy for the opening of the John F. Kennedy Center for the Performing Arts in Washington. In that piece, there is a scene that most of us can identify with. A priest celebrates a Roman Catholic Mass while dressed in layer upon layer of priestly vestments. In fact, his elegant embroidered robes are so heavy that he staggers under their weight. Those vestments represent layers of manmade rules and rituals and religious traditions, and it is obvious that those heavy layers of religiosity are destroying him and blocking his relationship with God.

Finally, the priest takes off the vestments and tosses them aside until he stands before God, clad only in blue jeans and T-shirt, and he approaches the altar and sings, "Look at me. There is nothing but me under this."

God sees through our façades, our false act of piety and religiosity, our plastic smile, our trappings of financial success and status. He wants us to throw aside all falsehood and religious performance and to just be who we are before him. He wants to liberate us from the bondage of keeping up with the Joneses and maintaining an appearance of status and success that we have not earned.

Be honest with God. Dethrone the false god of money, and give God first place in your life. Then experience the true liberation of serving God and God alone.

6

The Trap of Fatal Compromise

ron Eyes Cody was an Italian-American actor who portrayed Native Americans in films, TV shows, and commercials from the 1930s through the 1980s. You may remember his iconic scene with the tear rolling down his cheek in the "Keep America Beautiful" public service announcements on TV. In 1990, he retold an old legend in *Guideposts* to make an important point.

A long time ago, Native American youths would leave the village and seek solitude in the forest to prepare for their emergence into manhood. One young man hiked into a valley, where he fasted and meditated. Looking up toward the horizon, he saw the surrounding mountains with one tall, snow-capped peak. He decided to test himself against that forbidding mountain. Wearing a blanket and a buffalo hide for warmth, he climbed the mountain until he reached the top. From that peak, it seemed that he could see forever.

Then he heard a sound at his feet. Looking down, he saw a

rattlesnake. "I'm about to die," the snake said. "It's too cold for me here and I'm freezing. Put me under your shirt so that I can stay warm, and take me down to the valley and release me."

"No," the young man said. "I know your kind. You're a rattlesnake. If I pick you up, you'll bite me and I'll die."

"That's not so. I won't harm you. In fact, I'll be eternally grateful that you saved my life."

The young man resisted—but he felt sorry for the rattlesnake, and the snake was very persuasive. So, at last, he picked up the snake, tucked it under his shirt, and carried it down into the valley. As he was taking the rattlesnake out from under his shirt and lowering it toward the grass, the snake struck, biting the young man, injecting a lethal dose of venom.

"Why did you do that?" the young man cried out. "I saved your life! You promised you wouldn't bite me!"

"You knew what I was when you picked me up," the snake said as it slithered into the grass.[11]

The point of the story is clear. If you compromise with a rattlesnake, you can't complain if it bites you. Everybody knows what a rattlesnake is and what a rattlesnake does. You can't say, "That's not fair! You didn't play by the rules! It's not my fault!" None of that is true. Rattlesnakes play by their own rules, and if you let yourself be taken in by a snake, knowing full well that it's only natural and normal for snakes to bite, then whose fault is it that you got bitten? If you don't want to get bitten, stay clear of the snake's fangs.

This principle is equally true when the snake is Satan himself. When you compromise biblical principles, you expose yourself to Satan's moral and spiritual venom. You know that Satan is a snake—so keep your distance from him!

As the apostle Paul wrote to the Christians in Corinth, "But I am afraid that as the serpent deceived Eve by his cunning, your thoughts will be led astray from a sincere and pure devotion to Christ" (2 Corinthians 11:3). Be wise. Don't be deceived. Never compromise with the snake. Guard yourself against the venom of Satan.

An offer of compromise

In Nehemiah 6, we see three "rattlesnakes" who conspire against Nehemiah and his leadership. Their names are Sanballat, Tobiah, and Geshem the Arab. They plot against Nehemiah and try to entrap him, but Nehemiah knows a rattlesnake when he sees one, and he's wise enough not to pick one up. Nehemiah writes:

> Now when Sanballat and Tobiah and Geshem the Arab and the rest of our enemies heard that I had built the wall and that there was no breach left in it (although up to that time I had not set up the doors in the gates), Sanballat and Geshem sent to me, saying, "Come and let us meet together at Hakkephirim in the plain of Ono." But they intended to do me harm. And I sent messengers to them, saying, "I am doing a great work and I cannot come down. Why should the work stop while I leave it and come down to you?" And they sent to me four times in this way, and I answered them in the same manner (6:1-4).

Nehemiah's model of leadership makes us stop and take notice. Whether you are at the top of the corporate ladder or just stepping onto the first rung, this story is extremely instructive. Nehemiah's leadership example is relevant to us all. It's relevant to us dads and moms as leaders in the home. It's relevant to us as pastors, educators, business leaders, military leaders, or leaders in any other arena of life.

Nehemiah left the comfort and high position in the palace in Susa where he served as the chief of staff, the cupbearer to the king. God favored Nehemiah and gave him the king's ear so that Nehemiah was able to go Jerusalem, rally the people, and begin the rebuilding project. In the process, Nehemiah and his people faced continual opposition—some of it subtle, but most of it overt, involving ridicule, slander, intimidation, manipulation, lies, treachery, and fraud. All of these attacks were aimed at stopping the rebuilding project.

Finally, in Nehemiah 6, the enemies of the rebuilding project come to a conclusion. If they could not destroy God's work, then perhaps they could destroy God's worker. They would try to entice Nehemiah into a fatal compromise.

The reconstruction project was nearly finished, but it wasn't time for the ribbon-cutting ceremony. The walls were up, but the city gates had not yet been hung. As long as the city gates were wide open, Jerusalem was vulnerable to attack.

At this point, Sanballat and Company sent Nehemiah a message—or rather, four messages: Let's get together. Let's negotiate. Let's have a dialogue. Let's meet on the plains of Ono. They were saying, in effect, "Listen, Nehemiah, we may not have seen eye-to-eye recently, but let's let bygones be bygones. We don't need to be angry with each other. Come on, let's be friends."

The plains of Ono were located in a beautiful valley about twenty miles north of Jerusalem. The thought of a few days of relaxation in this resort-like valley might have seemed enticing for a man who had worked so hard with bricks, stones, and mortar.

Why did Sanballat suggest the plains of Ono as a meeting place? Because it was located about halfway between Jerusalem and Samaria. Sanballat was saying, in effect, "Let's compromise. You come halfway, we'll come halfway, and we'll meet in the middle." But Nehemiah wisely said, "Oh, no!" to Ono.

Now, the right kind of compromise is a good thing. Compromise is necessary to resolve conflicts in relationships, to negotiate contracts and business deals, and to make agreements between nations. In a good compromise, each side gives a little and gains a little so that all sides can come to agreement. Such compromises can be extremely helpful in maintaining peace and harmony in human relationships.

But in some areas of life we dare not compromise. We must not compromise biblical truth, biblical morality, and biblical ethics. When we compromise truth and values, we are compromising with Satan. We are compromising with the rattlesnake. We are taking the snake to our bosom—and when we compromise with a snake, we can never say later, "Why did the snake bite me?" We knew it was a snake when we picked it up.

Nehemiah knew that compromising with these snakes would be fatal. He knew that if he compromised with Sanballat, Tobiah, and Geshem, he could expect to get bitten. He refused to pick up the snake.

Wisdom and discernment

Compromise has ruined more churches than any other factor. Compromise has neutralized more preachers and wrecked more Christian lives than any other factor. Compromise would have led to the destruction of the wall around Jerusalem if Nehemiah had not been a wise and godly leader.

"Come down, Nehemiah," the rattlesnakes said. "Let's compromise. Let's talk it over. Let's come to a meeting of the minds." But Nehemiah said no—not just once but four times.

Over the years, I have been offered a number of compromises like the one these men offered to Nehemiah. I was once invited to join twenty religious leaders from various faith traditions to discuss human sexuality. I declined the invitation. The group invited me again, explaining, "You have a different point of view from most of the other participants. We want you to feel free to express your opinions."

I already knew that there would be, at most, two other participants who shared my biblical perspective on sexual ethics. And I knew that I was not being invited because they wanted to learn from me. They wanted me to learn from them. They wanted to criticize and marginalize my Scripture-based views. I declined a second time.

They contacted me again, and in their third invitation they said, "This will be a wonderful opportunity for you to discover new ideas and new points of view about human sexuality."

I declined a third time, saying, "I know all I need to know about human sexuality. I have the Scriptures as a guide to sexual ethics, and I have four children as proof that I have some practical knowledge of the subject."

If I had been younger, less mature, less spiritually discerning, I might have felt flattered at being invited to take part in such an event. But the Lord gave me discernment, and I realized that the agenda for the event had already been prepared, the conclusions had already been reached, and they wanted me there only so they could claim that a broad range of viewpoints were represented—and so they could browbeat the two or three token evangelicals for holding views they deemed to be narrow-minded and out of step with the times. I could tell it would be a waste of my time and energy at best and an ambush at worst.

At every decision point in our lives, we need to ask God for wisdom and discernment. The Lord gave discernment to Nehemiah, and Nehemiah had no doubt about the hidden intentions of Sanballat, Tobiah, and Geshem. So he replied to them, "I am doing a great work and I cannot come down. Why should the work stop while I leave it and come down to you?"

Nehemiah was not suggesting that the rebuilding project was a great work because *he* was doing it. He was saying it was a great work because *God* was doing it. When you obediently serve the Lord Jesus Christ and do the work he has assigned to you, then you can be assured that you are doing a great work. It doesn't matter whether you are building a church building, preaching sermons, teaching Sunday school, ushering, setting the communion table, or vacuuming the carpets after the worship service—if you are serving God, you are doing a great work. Don't ever compromise your work for the Lord.

And please understand, you don't have to be on church property to do the Lord's work. In fact, the most important work we do for God should take place out in the world, in the home, in the neighborhood, in the workplace, in the marketplace, on the campus, and wherever we come in contact with other people.

If you are a mother, don't ever say, "I am just a housewife, I'm just a mom." As a mother, you are shaping and instructing the children God has entrusted to you. You are raising them to know and serve God. You are training the next generation of Christian leaders. Moreover, you have a ministry to other mothers you meet at school, at dance classes and soccer games, in moms' support groups, and in the neighborhood. You have an outreach ministry to friends and neighbors. You have much more influence for Christ than you probably realize. If you make yourself available to him, you will be like Nehemiah, doing a great work.

Don't compromise the work you are doing for the Lord. Don't let other people deter you from serving him. Stay focused on your ministry for God and keep doing the great work he has given you to do. There are thousands of merely good works the world may try to draw you into. Stay focused on the *great* work of serving God.

One of my favorite intellectual pursuits is studying the theological and philosophical implications of the Wile E. Coyote and Road Runner cartoons. The Coyote is continually devising fiendish traps for the Road Runner, usually involving a complex device he has ordered from the Acme Corporation. The Coyote is persistent. He tries again and again to trap the Road Runner, but the Road Runner always escapes and always has the last "Beep-beep!"

Sanballat, Tobiah, and Geshem remind me of the Coyote—and I can just hear Nehemiah saying to them, "Beep-beep!" Four times Nehemiah says to them, "I will not come down. I will not give in. I will not capitulate. I will not compromise."

If Nehemiah had listened to Sanballat, Tobiah, and Geshem, if he had compromised with them and had ended up being ambushed by them, the entire project of rebuilding Jerusalem would have been sabotaged. Be wise like Nehemiah. Don't compromise with evil. Don't compromise the work God has given you to accomplish in his name.

From compromise to intimidation

In these days of opinion polls, focus groups, and Internet blogging, everyone has an *opinion* about everything. But very few people have *convictions*.

What is the difference between an opinion and a conviction? An opinion is a belief that *we hold*. A conviction is a belief that *holds us*. A conviction grips your mind and heart, and it will not let you go. Rarely would anyone be willing to suffer or die for an opinion. But down through the centuries, people have risked everything, even life itself, for their convictions. I believe that the times we live in demand that men and women of conviction stand up and be counted.

Daniel Webster was a brilliant American statesman and senator from Massachusetts who lived in momentous times during the nineteenth century. He was widely admired for his oratory, and one of his speeches, his "Reply to Hayne" in 1830, has been called the most eloquent speech ever delivered before Congress. In 1831, the poet Ralph Waldo Emerson wrote of him:

> Let Webster's lofty face
> Ever on thousands shine,
> A beacon set that Freedom's race
> Might gather omens from that radiant sign.

Webster was a staunchly antislavery senator with political aspirations to become president of the United States. In order to gain the nomination of his party, however, he compromised his views on slavery. He thought that by compromising, he would make himself more acceptable to those on both sides of the issue. Instead, voters rejected him for not standing firmly for his views. They saw Webster as lacking convictions, so his "radiant sign" was extinguished.

Twenty-three years after writing those original lines about Daniel Webster, Emerson offered this poetic assessment of his friend's character:

> Why did all manly gifts in Webster fail?
> He wrote on Nature's grandest brow "For Sale."

What a tragic epitaph for a once-promising life of leadership.

How many Christians have written "For Sale" on their brows, on their values, on their integrity, on their Christian testimony? In these days you will be tempted to compromise and sell out. Jesus said this would happen in the last days. You will be tempted to rethink what you believe about the Bible. You will be tempted to reevaluate your faith, your values, your commitments, your virtue, and your morality. You will be tempted to capitulate and compromise. Don't yield to that temptation. Stand firm like Nehemiah. When you are invited to compromise, say no. When you are asked again and again and again, say no, no, no, a thousand times no.

Nehemiah's enemies first tried to discourage Nehemiah with ridicule and mockery. Then they tried to entice Nehemiah with manipulation, wheedling, sweet talking, and cajoling. Neither their bullying nor their beguiling worked on Nehemiah. He refused to be distracted or deceived into compromising. His answer to all of their invitations was no, no, no, no.

So Nehemiah's enemies tried a new tactic, which we might call "An Open Letter to Nehemiah." Sanballat sent a servant to Nehemiah with a letter that read:

> In the same way Sanballat for the fifth time sent his servant to me with an open letter in his hand. In it was written, "It is reported among the nations, and Geshem also says it, that you and the Jews intend to rebel; that is why you are building the wall. And according to these reports you wish to become their king. And you have also set up prophets to proclaim concerning you in Jerusalem, 'There is a king in Judah.' And now the king will hear of these reports. So now come and let us take counsel together" (6:5-7).

Sanballat was clearly frustrated that his private overtures to Nehemiah had no effect, so now he decided to go public. He threatened to announce his accusations against Nehemiah—accusations that Nehemiah was ambitious to set himself up as a king in opposition to the king of Persia. Sanballat was essentially blackmailing Nehemiah, threatening to go to the king of Persia with these accusations if Nehemiah didn't agree to a meeting.

Appeals to compromise had failed. So Nehemiah's enemies resorted to intimidation, threatening to turn King Artaxerxes against Nehemiah with lies. Sanballat didn't spell out the consequences for Nehemiah if the Persian king believed those false accusations. The king would come against Nehemiah, capture him, torture him, and execute him as a rebel, making a public example of him—and he would destroy Jerusalem and slaughter the Jewish people as rebels.

Did Sanballat believe the accusation he threatened to make? Probably not. The godly character of Nehemiah was obvious for all to see. But Sanballat had constructed a deceitful yet plausible-sounding scenario to explain why Nehemiah was rebuilding the walls of Jerusalem. Sanballat was saying, in essence, "Nehemiah, you're an egomaniac, you're a wannabe dictator, you're an autocrat, you're in this for your own power and personal glory."

Nothing could be further from the truth. Nehemiah had left behind a position of power, comfort, and luxury in Susa. Now he was living in a sleeping bag, his life under constant threat, doing the work of a bricklayer, getting dirt under his fingernails and calluses on his hands, denying himself while encouraging others. And through it all, he had to endure the treacherous lies spread by Sanballat and his gossip machine.

We all know that people can't get enough of gossip. And the more evil and juicy the gossip, the quicker people are to believe it. We all know that gossip is a destructive force in families, neighborhoods, and workplaces. Unfortunately, gossip is also a destructive force in the church.

In Romans 1, the apostle Paul lists all kinds of evil done by people with "a debased mind"—people who are "full of envy, murder, strife, deceit, maliciousness. They are gossips, slanderers, haters of God, insolent, haughty, boastful, inventors of evil, disobedient to parents, foolish, faithless, heartless, ruthless" (Romans 1:29-31). And he warned Timothy about those in the church who go from house to house, stirring up trouble—"gossips and busybodies, saying what they should not" (1 Timothy 5:13). If you think gossip is a "minor sin" that God doesn't care about, think again. God's Word clearly states otherwise.

Nehemiah's enemies have threatened to use gossip to destroy his life and bring down the wrath of the Persians on the Jewish people. But Nehemiah is about to show us how a godly leader responds to opposition, intimidation, and threats of blackmail.

An assassination attempt

Nehemiah categorically denies Sanballat's false accusations. His conscience is clear and his life is an open book. Moreover, Nehemiah knows exactly what the motive is behind these charges:

> Then I sent to him, saying, "No such things as you say
> have been done, for you are inventing them out of your
> own mind." For they all wanted to frighten us, thinking,
> "Their hands will drop from the work, and it will not be
> done." But now, O God, strengthen my hands (6:8-9).

From time to time, everyone experiences criticism. Some of that criticism is false and unfair. But sometimes criticism is constructive and accurate, and at those times, we need to pay heed. None of us is perfect, and we all need other people in our lives to hold up a mirror to us and show us our faults and flaws so that we can make corrections. When criticism is fair-minded and justified, we need to stop being defensive, listen carefully, apologize quickly, ask to be forgiven, and then repent and move on.

But the criticism Sanballat leveled against Nehemiah was not true, not fair, not constructive, not accurate. False criticism is hard to defend against. It can sap your emotional energy and even your physical strength. It can cost you sleep. It can cause people to turn against you. It can destroy your reputation.

Whenever you are unfairly criticized and gossiped about, remind yourself of the words of the Lord Jesus when he said, "Blessed are you when others revile you and persecute you and utter all kinds of evil against you falsely on my account. Rejoice and be glad, for your reward is great in heaven, for so they persecuted the prophets who were before you" (Matthew 5:11-12).

That's the kind of criticism Nehemiah endured. His enemies had tried ridicule and mockery. Then they tried cajoling and compromising. Finally they tried intimidation. After all attempts failed to deter Nehemiah from his goal, his enemies tried yet one more approach:

> Now when I went into the house of Shemaiah the son of Delaiah, son of Mehetabel, who was confined to his home, he said, "Let us meet together in the house of God, within the temple. Let us close the doors of the temple, for they are coming to kill you. They are coming to kill you by night." But I said, "Should such a man as I run away? And what man such as I could go into the temple and live? I will not go in." And I understood and saw that God had not sent him, but he had pronounced the prophecy against me because Tobiah and Sanballat had hired him. For this purpose he was hired, that I should be afraid and act in this way and sin, and so they could give me a bad name in order to taunt me. Remember Tobiah and Sanballat, O

my God, according to these things that they did, and also
the prophetess Noadiah and the rest of the prophets who
wanted to make me afraid (6:10-14).

This final attack against Nehemiah involved an assassination
attempt. His enemies hired a false prophet, Shemaiah, who tried to
frighten Nehemiah into going alone to the temple. Shemaiah was a
sick man, confined to his bed, and he claimed to have a word from
the Lord—a message that Nehemiah's enemies were coming to kill
him and the only safe place would be in the temple. Neither Shemaiah nor Sanballat understood what made Nehemiah tick, because
he was *not* the kind of man to run from a fight.

When Shemaiah told Nehemiah that assassins were coming to
kill him, the news had the opposite of the intended effect. Nehemiah actually stiffened his resolve to stand his ground. In my favorite verse of the entire chapter, Nehemiah replied, "Should such a
man as I run away? And what man such as I could go into the temple and live? I will not go in."

The moment Nehemiah announced his intention to stand his
ground, the whole plot became clear to him. Nehemiah realized
that Shemaiah was a traitor not a prophet of God. Nehemiah had
learned to test the spirits. The Spirit of God had told Nehemiah to
stay, not to cut and run.

Nehemiah knew he should test Shemaiah's message against the
truth of God's Word. And God's Word made it clear that Nehemiah
was not to enter the holy place of the temple. No one but the Levit-
ical priests were allowed to enter that portion of the tabernacle and
later the temple. God's law said:

> "When the tabernacle is to set out, the Levites shall take
> it down, and when the tabernacle is to be pitched, the

Levites shall set it up. And if any outsider comes near, he
shall be put to death…

"And you shall appoint Aaron and his sons, and they shall
guard their priesthood. But if any outsider comes near,
he shall be put to death" (Numbers 1:51; 3:10).

Nehemiah was a layman, not a priest, and he could not go into
the sanctuary of the temple. He knew that any violation of this law
was punishable by death. Nehemiah had a refuge, but his refuge
was not the temple building. His refuge was God's Word and God's
authority.

The Lord of the impossible

Throughout all the opposition and persecution Nehemiah
endured from his enemies, he never sought revenge. He handed his
enemies over to the Lord to deal with according to his divine justice.
And God honored Nehemiah's faithfulness. In the closing verses
of Nehemiah 6, we see the outcome of the wall-building project
Nehemiah has led in obedience to God:

> So the wall was finished on the twenty-fifth day of the
> month Elul, in fifty-two days. And when all our enemies
> heard of it, all the nations around us were afraid and fell
> greatly in their own esteem, for they perceived that this
> work had been accomplished with the help of our God.
> Moreover, in those days the nobles of Judah sent many
> letters to Tobiah, and Tobiah's letters came to them. For
> many in Judah were bound by oath to him, because he
> was the son-in-law of Shecaniah the son of Arah: and his
> son Jehohanan had taken the daughter of Meshullam the
> son of Berechiah as his wife. Also they spoke of his good

deeds in my presence and reported my words to him. And
Tobiah sent letters to make me afraid (6:15-19).

At the beginning, the rebuilding of the wall had seemed to be
an impossible task, especially in the face of intense opposition. Yet
Nehemiah and the people of Judah, working in obedience to God's
plan, completed this impossible project in just fifty-two days. When
Nehemiah's enemies heard about it, they became disheartened and
discouraged. They realized that this was no mere human accom-
plishment. The rebuilding of the walls was achieved by the direct
intervention of the hand of God.

To the people, the task was impossible. But nothing is impossible for God. And nothing is impossible for God's people if they will
give God the credit and the glory.

What was true in Nehemiah's day is still true today. We serve the
same God Nehemiah served. We face daunting challenges and fierce
opposition, just as Nehemiah did. We live in a post-Christian world.
Militant Islam, militant secularism, and militant atheism are on the
move, and Western civilization is in decline. Christianity appears to
be in eclipse—but that is only institutional Christianity, what we
might call "churchianity."

True Christianity, the Christianity that Jesus taught, that Paul
spread throughout the Gentile world, that the early church exemplified, that the Reformers purified, that the persecuted church has
kept alive behind the Iron and Bamboo Curtains—that kind of obedient, risky, bold, brawny Christianity is still alive and well and on
the move. Persecution may come to the Western world. Some so-
called Christians of superficial faith will wither and fall away, but
authentic followers of Christ will endure to the end.

Let all the world know that we serve the Lord of the impossible.

When he gives us an impossible assignment, we will accomplish it by his power, and we will say, "God did it!" We will not compromise with evil. We will not be fooled by the snake. We will not be intimidated by the enemy.

Like Nehemiah, we will stand firm. We will raise the walls. Our only refuge will be God's Word and God's authority. All praise and glory be to God as he leads us in victory.

7

The Four Secrets of Renewal and Revival

A writer once described a new disease that afflicts many professing Christians: *Morbus Sundayitis*—or in layman's language, "Sunday sickness." The symptoms vary, though the illness never seems to be accompanied by a loss of appetite. The illness always sets in on Sunday morning, just before time to leave for church. The illness always runs its course by about half past twelve, in time for the sufferer to enjoy a hearty lunch and an afternoon of golf or watching football on TV. The symptoms do not return until the following Sunday.

All too often in our culture, we view time spent worshiping the Lord as an unpleasant chore to be avoided. But in the next section of Nehemiah, we will see that Nehemiah and his people viewed worship as an experience of joy—a privilege they eagerly anticipated. By understanding how Nehemiah and the people of Jerusalem viewed worship, we will begin to see worship in a whole new way.

As we come to this passage, the walls are completed and the gates are hung. The Jewish people, under the direction of God, have completed this construction project in a mere fifty-two days. In spite of opposition, threats, and difficulties caused by their enemies, the people of God have completed the task.

But Nehemiah understands the walls are just walls, gates are just gates, and buildings are just buildings. They are mere objects made of wood and stone. What matters to Nehemiah is not the structures themselves but the use God's people will make of the structures. What matters to Nehemiah is not so much the building of the edifice but the edification of the builders. He is intensely interested in the revival of the hearts of the people after the building is finished. With eyes of faith, he could see revival coming.

Nehemiah didn't envision the people of Jerusalem serving a building. Rather, he saw the building as a place where the people would serve God and God would bless the people. He saw the restoration of Jerusalem as an occasion of great joy. And that is why, in Nehemiah 8, he tells the people to celebrate: "Go your way. Eat the fat and drink sweet wine and send portions to anyone who has nothing ready, for this day is holy to our Lord. And do not be grieved, for the joy of the LORD is your strength" (8:10).

Do you want a blueprint for joy in your life? Do you want a formula for renewal and growth? Do you want to understand the secret of godly contentment and confidence?

Nehemiah reveals all of that and more to us in Nehemiah 7 and 8. In the coming pages we will discover the secrets to renewal and revival—powerful life lessons that Nehemiah exemplifies in this passage. Those secrets are:

1. *Assembling* together with other believers.

2. *Affirming* the authority of God's Word.

3. *Adoring* the God of grace.

4. *Honoring* God by surrendering all to him.

If we truly grasp the practical power of these four principles, we will be renewed and reenergized to impact the world for God in the twenty-first century.

Principle 1: Assembling together with other believers

As Nehemiah 7 opens, we see that the goal of rebuilding the walls is completed—but this is only the first phase of the rebuilding project. Nehemiah writes:

> Now when the wall had been built and I had set up the doors, and the gatekeepers, the singers, and the Levites had been appointed, I gave my brother Hanani and Hananiah the governor of the castle charge over Jerusalem, for he was a more faithful and God-fearing man than many. And I said to them, "Let not the gates of Jerusalem be opened until the sun is hot. And while they are still standing guard, let them shut and bar the doors. Appoint guards from among the inhabitants of Jerusalem, some at their guard posts and some in front of their own homes." The city was wide and large, but the people within it were few, and no houses had been rebuilt (7:1-4).

At this point, the city of Jerusalem is not really a city at all in the conventional sense. It is an enclosure, a walled fortress—but the homes and shops and other structures that were destroyed decades earlier by the soldiers of Nebuchadnezzar have still not been rebuilt.

At this point, Nehemiah appoints officials to govern the city and sets guards on the walls and the gates.

In the rest of the chapter 7, Nehemiah—as directed by God—gathers the nobles, the officials, and the people so that their names can be registered by family groupings. The chapter goes on to list the names of those families that returned to Jerusalem from exile in Babylon, along with the names of the priests and Levites, the temple singers, the gatekeepers, and the servants. The total enrollment came to approximately fifty thousand people.

Then, in Nehemiah 8, we read:

> And all the people gathered as one man into the square before the Water Gate. And they told Ezra the scribe to bring the Book of the Law of Moses that the LORD had commanded Israel. So Ezra the priest brought the Law before the assembly, both men and women and all who could understand what they heard, on the first day of the seventh month (8:1-2).

All the people gathered at the place of assembly, the square at the Water Gate. There, Ezra the scribe read from the book of the Law of Moses.

Why is it important for God's people to gather together? Many people say, "I can worship God just as well on the golf course or in the mountains as I can in church." Well, there is a small kernel of truth in that statement. We can worship God wherever we are, even if we are stuck in a traffic jam or sitting in the dentist's chair. God is always available to us, and we can talk to him, praise him, sing spiritual songs of worship to him, and listen for his voice.

But it's not true that worshiping God in the privacy of our thoughts is the equivalent of gathering with other believers and worshiping God as one. When believers assemble together and unite their hearts in prayer and praise and worship, something mystical and even miraculous takes place. Jesus said, "Again I say to you, if two of you agree on earth about anything they ask, it will be done for them by my Father in heaven. For where two or three are gathered in my name, there am I among them" (Matthew 18:19-20).

The writer of the New Testament book of Hebrews warns against neglecting the habit of assembling together to worship the Lord: "And let us consider how to stir up one another to love and good works, not neglecting to meet together, as is the habit of some, but encouraging one another, and all the more as you see the Day drawing near" (Hebrews 10:24-25).

If you are a spiritually sensitive Christian, and you have ever been unable to attend church for a length of time, you know that your heart for God grows colder the longer you stay away. And when you return, just being among God's people, worshiping the Lord and singing spiritual songs, brings a thrill to your heart.

I was a teenager when I committed my life to the Lord, and I was immediately on fire to serve him. I would share the good news of Jesus Christ with anyone without hesitation. But though I was eager to witness for Christ, I did not want a career as a pastor. When I became aware that God was calling me into full-time Christian ministry, I rebelled against the Lord. Like the prophet Jonah in the Old Testament, I wandered far away from God. I dropped out of the church, and I lost the joy of knowing and serving my Lord Jesus Christ for about a year and a half. But my loving sister refused to give up on me. She prayed for me and patiently but persistently helped me find my way back into the fellowship of the church.

God didn't design us to be Lone Ranger Christians. He created us to be in community together. We need each other in the body of

Christ. When we gather together with other believers, we encourage one another, support one another, and challenge one another to a deeper faith experience. One person alone can sing a song of praise to the Lord, but a roomful of voices becomes a symphony of praise.

In *Moments for Each Other*, Robert Strand tells the story of Linda, a young woman traveling alone in a little Honda Civic toward Whitehorse in the Yukon Territory. She had never traveled so far north before, and didn't know that she was heading into four-wheel-drive territory. She spent the night in a small lodge beside the rugged highway, then got up early in the morning to continue her trip. Stepping out of her cabin, she found the entire landscape shrouded in fog.

Linda went to the small coffee shop for breakfast, and a couple of truckers asked her where she was headed in that little compact car.

"Whitehorse," she said.

The truckers shook their heads. One of them said, "You'll never reach Whitehorse in weather like this."

"Well, I'm determined to try," Linda replied.

"In that case," one trucker said, "we're just going to have to hug you."

"Oh, no you don't!" Linda said. "Don't you touch me!"

The truckers laughed. "You don't understand. 'Hugging' means we put one truck in front of you and one behind you. That way, we can make sure you make it safely to Whitehorse."

So Linda let the two truckers "hug" her car. She followed the taillights of the lead truck, and the headlights in her rearview mirror assured her that, no matter what happened, help was close at hand. And she made it safely to Whitehorse.[12]

That is what Christians do for each other in the church. We "hug" each other along our journey together and help each other to arrive safely at our destination with the Lord. Our brothers and sisters in Christ get us through the foggy, treacherous, slippery passes of life. Some lead the way. Others keep a close watch on us. That's an excellent picture of close Christian fellowship.

Wise King Solomon put it this way: "Two are better than one, because they have a good reward for their toil. For if they fall, one will lift up his fellow. But woe to him who is alone when he falls and has not another to lift him up!" (Ecclesiastes 4:9-10).

Principle 2: Affirming the authority of God's Word

Why do we gather regularly as believers? Is it merely to experience that warm, fuzzy feeling of togetherness? There's nothing wrong with warm, fuzzy feelings, but feelings don't last long. We gather together to experience the awe of joining our hearts together in worship and reverence of our Almighty God. We gather together to join our hearts together in prayer to him. And we gather together to hear God speak to us through the reading and preaching of his Word.

And that's what took place in the public square next to the Water Gate in the city of Jerusalem. The people assembled to hear Ezra the scribe read the Word of God.

> And he read from it facing the square before the Water Gate from early morning until midday, in the presence of the men and the women and those who could understand. And the ears of all the people were attentive to the Book of the Law. And Ezra the scribe stood on a wooden platform that they had made for the purpose. And beside him stood Mattithiah, Shema, Anaiah, Uriah, Hilkiah, and Maaseiah on his right hand, and Pedaiah, Mishael, Malchijah, Hashum, Hashbaddanah, Zechariah,

and Meshullam on his left hand. And Ezra opened the book in the sight of all the people, for he was above all the people, and as he opened it all the people stood. And Ezra blessed the LORD, the great God, and all the people answered, "Amen, Amen," lifting up their hands. And they bowed their heads and worshiped the LORD with their faces to the ground. Also Jeshua, Bani, Sherebiah, Jamin, Akkub, Shabbethai, Hodiah, Maaseiah, Kelita, Azariah, Jozabad, Hanan, Pelaiah, the Levites, helped the people to understand the Law, while the people remained in their places. They read from the book, from the Law of God, clearly, and they gave the sense, so that the people understood the reading (8:3-8).

So Ezra unrolled the book of the Law of Moses, and all the thousands of people who filled that square joined their hearts and listened to the Word of God. And there were many priests on hand to interpret and explain the Law of Moses, so that the people could clearly understand God's Word.

In order for revival to take place in one life, or in the life of a church, or in the life of a nation, it must begin with a hunger and thirst for the Word of God. There are millions of Bibles in homes, libraries, and churches across our land. Most Christians own numerous copies of the Bible in an assortment of translations. If you have a computer, tablet, or smartphone, you can read the Bible in any translation for free on the Internet, along with commentaries and concordances and every Bible study help imaginable. Ironically, however, most people (including most Christians) know very little about the Bible.

The Bible is not just a collection of old stories and inspirational quotations. It is the guidebook to victorious living in Christ—and it is the key that unlocks the door to revival. Until churches boldly proclaim the Word of God and Christians obey it, there will never be revival and healing in our land.

Here in Nehemiah 8, we see the people of Jerusalem preparing the way for revival. They have assembled to hear and affirm the Word of God. They don't merely affirm it as a good book, an instructional book, or an inspiring book. They affirm it as the authoritative Word of God.

I used to take it for granted that those who call themselves evangelical Christians accepted God's Word as having authority over every area of their lives. A number of years ago, however, a man sat in my office who had been a member of our church for three years. He said to me, "The Bible is not relevant to today's problems." Since then, I have heard other "evangelical Christians," including some who are pastors and Christian authors, say much the same thing.

But when Ezra preached the Word of God to the people of Jerusalem, he not only read it, but he and his fellow priests expounded and exposited the Scriptures. They explained what God's Word said, what it meant, and how it applied to the practical realities of the lives of God's people.

When I preach and teach God's Word in my church or in books like this one, I try to follow the model of Ezra. I don't preach moralistic sermons, designed merely to help people treat each other more nicely. I don't preach psychological sermons, designed merely to improve people's happiness and self-esteem. I don't preach humanistic sermons, designed to help people become more tolerant and progressive. I don't preach social gospel sermons, designed to affect social policy by pitting class against class.

I preach the Word of God. I present the Word of God. When necessary, I study God's Word in the original Hebrew, Aramaic, or

Greek language to explore the richness of its meaning. I explain it and apply its truths to everyday life.

It's important to notice this statement in verse 5: "And Ezra opened the book in the sight of all the people, for he was above all the people, and as he opened it all the people stood." The people had such a deep reverence for the Word of God that they rose to their feet as Ezra opened the Book of the Law. This is a sign of deep affirmation and respect for God's Word.

In verse 6, we see a similar sign: "And Ezra blessed the LORD, the great God, and all the people answered, 'Amen, Amen,' lifting up their hands." When Ezra blessed and praised God, the people joined him with upraised hands and a huge outpouring of emotion.

Many Christians today treat the Bible as a buffet table from which they choose what they like and pass by what they dislike. Some say, "I don't like what the Bible says about judgment and hell." Some say, "I don't like what the Bible says about sexual ethics, marriage, and homosexuality." Some say, "I don't like what the Bible says about tithing and giving and the way I use my money." When people think they have a right to critique God's Word, to judge certain portions as no longer valid, to reject this book or that passage, they have set themselves up as judges over God himself. The psalmist wrote,

> I bow down toward your holy temple and give thanks
> to your name for your steadfast love and your
> faithfulness,
> for you have exalted above all things
> your name and your word.
> (Psalm 138:2)

We often say that a man's name is as good as his word. The same is true of God. His name, his character, and his nature are as good as his Word. He has exalted his name and his Word above all things. That's why the Bible is a perfect book.

The Bible needs no editing or revising because it is not a human-made book. Because it is inspired by God, the Bible has a perfect answer to every situation in our lives. The Bible is pure, without contradiction. Examine any church where the leaders have fallen into sin and where the ministry has begun to crumble, and you almost always find that those leaders have compromised the authority of God's Word. Churches that subordinate the Word of God to human reason, to human experience, to political fads, or to cultural fashion are churches that have begun to doubt and deny the Word of God.

Those churches will not be blessed by God. He has promised to bless the faithful preaching of his Word. Only through the preaching of God's Word can we know the God who is revealed in his Word. Whenever the Word is taught, read, or preached, Jesus steps out of the pages of the book and we meet him face to face. And when we meet Jesus, he transforms our lives.

If we want revival in our lives, in our churches, and in our nation, we must begin by assembling together around God's Word, and we must affirm the authority of his Word over every aspect of our lives.

Principle 3: Adoring the God of grace

The people stood in the square, surrounded by the freshly reconstructed fortress walls of Jerusalem. As recorded in the book of Ezra, the temple had been rebuilt. But the houses and shops were still in ruins, destroyed by the Babylonians under Nebuchadnezzar. God had allowed the Babylonians to take the Jewish nation into exile because of the disobedience and spiritual adultery of the people. As Ezra read the Book of the Law to the people, they remembered the disobedience of their nation—and they wept:

> And Nehemiah, who was the governor, and Ezra the priest
> and scribe, and the Levites who taught the people said to
> all the people, "This day is holy to the LORD your God; do
> not mourn or weep." For all the people wept as they heard
> the words of the Law. Then he said to them, "Go your way.
> Eat the fat and drink sweet wine and send portions to
> anyone who has nothing ready, for this day is holy to our
> Lord. And do not be grieved, for the joy of the LORD is your
> strength." So the Levites calmed all the people, saying,
> "Be quiet, for this day is holy; do not be grieved." And all
> the people went their way to eat and drink and to send
> portions and to make great rejoicing, because they had
> understood the words that were declared to them (8:9-12).

The people rightly mourned the sin and disobedience that had brought destruction on the holy city and exile to the nation of Israel. But Ezra and Nehemiah said to the people, "This day is holy to the LORD your God; do not mourn or weep...for the joy of the LORD is your strength." Those words lifted the hearts of the people, and they understood the message of grace and forgiveness that had been declared to them.

The Word of God had pierced their hearts with grief—but the Word of God had also brought repentance to their hearts and an understanding that they served a God of grace. Once they had repented of their sin, it was time to adore God, rejoice in his strength, and celebrate his goodness, mercy, and amazing grace.

Sincere grief and repentance from sin is always followed by great joy. You cannot experience the authentic joy of the Lord until you have expressed sorrow over your sin. The Word of God must penetrate your heart and stir up repentance in order for the joy of the Lord to lift your spirit to the heavens.

Jesus said, "These things I have spoken to you, that my joy may be in you, and that your joy may be full" (John 15:11). Have you experienced the joy of the Lord? You cannot explain his joy; you can only experience it. And once you have experienced it, you cannot help adoring the God of grace.

Authentic joy and true contentment do not come from outward experiences, such as winning the lottery or taking a dream vacation. Outward circumstances may bring you momentary happiness and tragic events may steal your happiness away. But authentic joy and true contentment cannot be stolen from you by a financial setback, the betrayal of a friend, or a troubling diagnosis. Authentic joy is a gift from God, and it comes straight from his Word. It's a gift no one can take from you. As the psalmist reminds us:

> The precepts of the LORD are right,
>   rejoicing the heart;
> the commandment of the LORD is pure,
>   enlightening the eyes.
>   (Psalm 19:8)

Principle 4: Honoring God by surrendering all to him

In the concluding verses of Nehemiah 8, we see the people honoring God by heeding his Word and surrendering to him:

On the second day the heads of fathers' houses of all the people, with the priests and the Levites, came together to Ezra the scribe in order to study the words of the Law. And they found it written in the Law that the LORD had commanded by Moses that the people of Israel should dwell in booths during the feast of the seventh month, and that they should proclaim it and publish it in all their towns and in Jerusalem, "Go out to the hills and bring branches of olive, wild olive, myrtle, palm, and other leafy trees to make booths, as it is written." So the people went out and brought them and made booths for themselves, each on his roof, and in their courts and in the courts of the house of God, and in the square at the Water Gate and in the square at the Gate of Ephraim. And all the assembly of those who had returned from the captivity made booths and lived in the booths, for from the days of Jeshua the son of Nun to that day the people of Israel had not done so. And there was very great rejoicing. And day by day, from the first day to the last day, he read from the Book of the Law of God. They kept the feast seven days, and on the eighth day there was a solemn assembly, according to the rule (8:13-18).

When Ezra read from the Book of the Law of God, the people rediscovered one of the requirements of the Law, the Feast of Booths (or Feast of Tabernacles), which is described in Leviticus 23:33-44. This feast, celebrated on the fifteenth day of the month of Tishrei (in September or October on our calendars) lasts seven days. It is named for the booths or tabernacles (Hebrew *sukkōt*; fragile and temporary dwellings often covered with palm branches) that resemble the dwellings of the Israelites during their forty years of wandering after they left Egypt.

After Ezra read to them, the people committed themselves to keeping this provision of the Law of Moses. They reinstituted the Feast of Booths, and they went out into the hills to gather leafy branches and they made booths to dwell in during the Feast. They set aside seven days to devote themselves to the Lord, and each day Ezra read to the people from the Law. Then, on the eighth day, they gathered for a sacred and solemn assembly.

During that time, the people of Israel *heard* the Word of God, they *honored* the Word of God, they *heeded* the Word of God, and they *put God's Word into action*. This is what authentic revival looks like. The people consecrated themselves to God, set themselves apart for God, and surrendered themselves completely to God.

When the people heard God's Word and obeyed it, they experienced the joy of the Lord. They began to revel in God's grace and enjoy their faith once more. And that is God's goal for your life and mine—to enjoy our faith and to experience the joy of a vital relationship with him.

When you are out of the will of God, when you're out of fellowship with God, you can still put on your Sunday clothes, paste on your Sunday smile, and sing hymns and pretend you mean the words—but church will be drudgery for you. Being with other Christians will hold no joy for you. Wearing a pious mask and pretending to be something you're not is exhausting.

But living authentically for the Lord is empowering. When you hear God's Word and obey it, the joy of the Lord will be your strength. When you surrender everything you are, you gain everything God is. So honor God, receive his grace, surrender to his will, and experience his joy!

8

Confession and Commitment

r. Frederick Edward Marsh (1858–1931) was a great Bible teacher and a prolific author. On one occasion, he preached a sermon on the confession of sin. Afterward, a young man, a member of the church, approached him with a troubled expression.

"Pastor," the young man said, "your sermon has put me in a terrible dilemma."

"How so?"

"I am a boat builder by trade, and I work for a man who's not a Christian. I have often tried to witness to him, and I've been encouraging him to come to church and hear you preach. He wants nothing to do with Christ, and he scoffs at all my attempts to witness to him. But Pastor, I've done something terrible. I need to go confess it to my employer—but if I tell them what I did, my testimony will be ruined forever."

"What did you do?"

"In my spare time, I've been building a boat for myself in my own yard. We boat builders use copper nails because they don't rust. The problem is that copper nails are very expensive—and I've been pocketing copper nails at work and bringing them home to use on my own boat."

"I see."

"I tried to rationalize what I did. I told myself that my employer would never miss a few nails. And besides, he really ought to pay me more than he does. But as I listened to your sermon today, I realized that stealing those nails from work made me nothing but a common thief. I have no excuse for what I did."

"In that case," Dr. Marsh said, "there is only one thing to do. You must confess what you did and pay for the nails you took."

"But don't you see? I *can't* do that! I've been witnessing to him. I've been telling him that knowing Jesus Christ as my Lord and Savior has made a difference in my life. If I admit that I stole from him, he'll think I was just a hypocrite. Yet those copper nails are digging into my conscience, and I'll never have peace until I put this matter right."

"The Bible makes it clear what you must do—and so does your conscience. You don't really need me to tell you what you have to do now."

"I know you're right, Pastor," the young man said. "I just don't think I can bring myself to do it." And with that, he walked out of the church.

A few weeks later, the young man returned to the church and approached Dr. Marsh after the service. The young man smiled broadly, and it seemed a huge weight had been lifted from his shoulders.

"Pastor," he said, "I settled the matter of the copper nails and my conscience is relieved at last."

"What did your employer say when you confessed the theft to him?"

"That's the amazing thing," the young man said. "When I told him what I had done, he looked at me strangely and said, 'I've always thought of you as just another religious hypocrite. I've met so many phonies claiming to be Christians, and I thought you were one of those. But any faith that would cause a young man to confess to stealing copper nails and offer to make restitution—well, that's a faith worth looking into.'"[13]

Unconfessed sin weighs us down and takes the joy out of our lives. God can't use us as his witnesses when we are living a lie. But when we are truly repentant, when we confess our sins to those we have wronged and to God himself, God not only restores our joy, but he also is able to use us to spread his good news.

Here in Nehemiah 9, we see that the people of Israel respond to the reading of God's Word by coming together to confess their sins. When we truly receive and understand the Word of God, it drives us to our knees, it drives us to God in prayer, and it compels us to confess our sins and repent. The Word of God alters our priorities and leads us to a deeper commitment to God.

The cleansing of confession

Nehemiah 9 contains the longest prayer recorded in the Bible. It is a prayer of confession—and a prayer of commitment:

> Now on the twenty-fourth day of this month the people of Israel were assembled with fasting and in sackcloth, and with earth on their heads. And the Israelites separated themselves from all foreigners and stood and confessed their sins and the iniquities of their fathers. And they stood up in their place and read from the Book of the Law of the

LORD their God for a quarter of the day; for another quarter
of it they made confession and worshiped the LORD their
God (9:1-3).

Confession is a cleansing act. The people began their prayer by
confessing their own sin and by worshiping and giving reverence to
God. They came before God with fasting, clad in the sackcloth of
humility, with the dust of the earth sprinkled on their heads to symbolize their lowliness before God. They came in brokenness before
God. They came in sincerity. They came in confession and repentance. The people of Israel understood that it was impossible to
receive God's forgiveness without sincere confession and repentance.

We cannot receive salvation until we recognize and acknowledge
our hopelessness and lostness apart from Jesus Christ. Once we confess that we can never live up to God's standard of righteousness,
once we admit that we cannot fix our sinfulness by our own efforts
and in our own strength, once we accept our brokenness and we surrender to God, we are ready to receive God's salvation.

We must come to the end of ourselves and say, "Lord, you are my
only hope. You are the One who paid for my sin on the cross. You are
the only One who can help me face the endless eternity." Until we
come before God clad in the sackcloth of humility, with the dust of
repentance on our heads, we cannot receive the salvation Jesus offers
us. We must come to the Lord in the spirit expressed by the psalmist:

> Have mercy on me, O God,
>   according to your steadfast love;
> according to your abundant mercy
>   blot out my transgressions.
> Wash me thoroughly from my iniquity,
>   and cleanse me from my sin!...

Purge me with hyssop, and I shall be clean;
 wash me, and I shall be whiter than snow.
Let me hear joy and gladness;
 let the bones that you have broken rejoice.
Hide your face from my sins,
 and blot out all my iniquities.
Create in me a clean heart, O God,
 and renew a right spirit within me.
Cast me not away from your presence,
 and take not your Holy Spirit from me.
Restore to me the joy of your salvation,
 and uphold me with a willing spirit.
 (Psalm 51:1-2,7-12)

Don't ever mistake brokenness for weakness. Only a truly broken spirit can receive strength from the Lord. God is near to those who are crushed in spirit.

The people of Israel are humble, broken, crushed in spirit, and repentant. But they don't stop with confession and repentance. This prayer is not a general statement such as, "God, you're so great and we are so unworthy." No, these people meant business with God. They had gathered to make a commitment to God, a promise to completely alter their priorities, and to devote themselves to God in a new way. To demonstrate to God that they truly meant business with him, they signed their names on the dotted line at the end of that prayer (see 9:38).

Authentic commitment versus "easy believism"

We live in a world that is commitment-phobic. Our generation takes commitment lightly. Few people in our culture have a sense of duty or honor toward the promises they make. They say, "Yes, I remember I promised at the altar 'as long as we both shall live.' But that was then. This is now." Some couples, recognizing they have no intention of keeping the marriage commitment for life, have actually reworded the promise clause of the marriage vow to read "as long as we both shall *love*"—which is no promise, no commitment whatsoever.

In America, we don't even believe in making a commitment to the church. We are church shoppers and church hoppers. We shop for churches the way we shop for cars, looking for the particular features we like and that will make us feel good. If, after a while, we realize that we don't like our church as much as we thought we would, if our church isn't entertaining enough, if the sermons don't always make us feel good about ourselves, we trade that church in on a different model.

All too many people select their church on the basis of "What will this church do for me?" rather than "Does this church preach the Word of God?" and "Is this church committed to biblical authority?" Too many people are looking for a church that will cater to their "easy believism" instead of challenging them to a deeper spiritual maturity and a closer walk with God.

An equally serious problem is that many churches and pastors are scrambling to appeal to this constituency and are trying to market the gospel of Jesus Christ as if it were a product to be sold. No wonder the church in America is in a spiritual crisis. Instead of challenging the culture, the church today largely reflects the insipid values and commitment phobia of our dying society.

The people in Nehemiah's day had already experienced the death of their culture. They had seen Israel decay to a point where God had to use the wicked Babylonians to chastise the nation and bring the people to their senses. They had spent more than seven decades in exile in an alien land. They had no desire to undergo the horrors of that exile once more.

The people of Israel were now committed to God. They were eager to sign and seal their commitment with their names and their own lives. So, as Nehemiah goes on to tell us, the Levites called upon the people to bless and praise God and led the people in the following prayer:

> "Stand up and bless the LORD your God from everlasting to everlasting. Blessed be your glorious name, which is exalted above all blessing and praise.

> "You are the LORD, you alone. You have made heaven, the heaven of heavens, with all their host, the earth and all that is on it, the seas and all that is in them; and you preserve all of them; and the host of heaven worships you. You are the LORD, the God who chose Abram and brought him out of Ur of the Chaldeans and gave him the name Abraham. You found his heart faithful before you, and made with him the covenant to give to his offspring the land of the Canaanite, the Hittite, the Amorite, the Perizzite, the Jebusite, and the Girgashite. And you have kept your promise, for you are righteous" (9:5-8).

This part of the prayer focuses on the glory of God and the faithfulness of God. It extols God as the Maker of heaven and earth, and the One the host of heaven worships. This portion of the prayer also recalls how God made a covenant with Abraham and his descendants. God was faithful even when God's people were unfaithful. He kept his side of the bargain even when the Hebrew people broke theirs.

Cycles of blessing and defection

In verses 9 to 25, the prayer goes on to recount how the Hebrew people suffered affliction and slavery in Egypt, yet God, through Moses, performed signs and wonders against Pharaoh. Our God is the "can-do God" who brought the Hebrew people out of Egypt, parted the sea before them, led them through the desert, gave them the Law at Mount Sinai, and fed them with bread from heaven in the wilderness.

The prayer also confesses that the people became presumptuous and disobedient. Yet even when they sinned against God, he was ready to forgive them. In his mercy, he did not forsake them. God forgave them, sustained them, led them, and provided for them. And the people entered the Promised Land, subdued the pagan Canaanite people, possessed the land, and multiplied. The people of Israel lived in a rich land, enjoying the vineyards, olive orchards, and fruit trees of the land as a gift of God's grace. Even so, the prayer continues, we see that all did not go well with the people of Israel:

> "Nevertheless, they were disobedient and rebelled against you and cast your law behind their back and killed your prophets, who had warned them in order to turn them back to you, and they committed great blasphemies. Therefore you gave them into the hand of their enemies, who made them suffer. And in the time of their suffering they cried out to you and you heard them from heaven, and according to your great mercies you gave them saviors who saved them from the hand of their enemies. But after they had rest they did evil again before you, and you abandoned them to the hand of their enemies, so that they had dominion over them. Yet when they turned and cried to you, you heard from heaven, and many

times you delivered them according to your mercies. And you warned them in order to turn them back to your law. Yet they acted presumptuously and did not obey your commandments, but sinned against your rules, which if a person does them, he shall live by them, and they turned a stubborn shoulder and stiffened their neck and would not obey. Many years you bore with them and warned them by your Spirit through your prophets. Yet they would not give ear. Therefore you gave them into the hand of the peoples of the lands. Nevertheless, in your great mercies you did not make an end of them or forsake them, for you are a gracious and merciful God" (9:26-31).

In this part of the prayer, the people bless the Lord for being a just and holy God. Because of their rebellion and sin, the people needed to be corrected and disciplined by God. So the Lord delivered the Jewish people into the hands of their enemies—not because God hated them or wanted to get even with them, but because he loved them and wanted to restore them to himself. When they repented, God brought them back into their land and enabled them to rebuild Jerusalem.

Our God is a glorious God, a faithful God, a mighty God, a generous God, and a forgiving and pardoning God. But we must never forget that our God is a holy God. He loves us too much to let us wallow in our sin. God doesn't want to afflict us, but if we insist on it through our rebellion, God will use affliction in our lives to draw us back to himself.

God brought the people of Israel out of bondage in Egypt and fed them manna, the bread of heaven, in the wilderness. How did God's people respond to his grace? "But they and our fathers acted presumptuously and stiffened their neck and did not obey your commandments" (9:16). For forty years, the Lord sustained the people in the wilderness, then he led them over the River Jordan and into the Promised Land. There God blessed them and gave them fortified cities and rich land. How did God's people respond to his grace? "Nevertheless, they were disobedient and rebelled against you and cast your law behind their back and killed your prophets, who had warned them in order to turn them back to you, and they committed great blasphemies" (9:26).

Then came the time of the judges. For more than three centuries, Israel went through the same cycle again and again: First, the Jewish people enjoyed a time of spiritual blessing. Then they descended into spiritual defection and defeat. This was followed by God's discipline when he handed the people over to their enemies. Then the people would repent and cry out to God for deliverance. Finally, God in his mercy would send Israel a judge, a deliverer. This would result in another time of blessing, and the cycle would begin all over again.

What was the result of all these cycles during the time of the judges? How did the people respond to God's grace? "Many times you delivered them according to your mercies. And you warned them in order to turn them back to your law. Yet they acted presumptuously and did not obey your commandments...and they turned a stubborn shoulder and stiffened their neck and would not obey" (9:28b-29).

In spite of all these acts of rebellion and spiritual defection, God remained steadfast in his love and mercy. The prayer continues: "Nevertheless, in your great mercies you did not make an end of them or forsake them, for you are a gracious and merciful God" (9:31). You would think that the people would respond positively to the grace and mercy of God. But no. Once God had answered their prayers and delivered them, they forgot all about God.

I once heard a story told by a postal clerk in the dead-letter office in Washington, DC. He studied the mail that came in during the Christmas season. Prior to Christmas Day, thousands of letters arrived addressed to Santa Claus with many requests for toys and gifts. After Christmas, however, only one postcard arrived, thanking Santa Claus for the gifts that had been delivered on Christmas Day.

As we look through the books from Exodus through Judges, and we see how the Jewish people responded to God's grace again and again with ingratitude, rebellion, and disobedience, we might be tempted to judge the people harshly. We might wonder, "Why were the people of ancient Israel so wayward and disobedient? I would never behave that way."

Don't be so sure. The people of ancient Israel are no different from you and me. This story of blessing followed by defection is the story of humanity in a microcosm. This is a picture of how human beings universally behave in response to God's love and grace. We all rebel. We all break his commandments. As the prophet Jeremiah wrote,

> The heart is deceitful above all things,
>   and desperately sick;
> who can understand it?
>   (Jeremiah 17:9)

If you look back over your own history, you can undoubtedly remember times when you took God's grace for granted, when you responded to his kindness and mercy with sin and rebellion, when you responded to his love with stubbornness. Many times you have deserved discipline from the Lord, yet he has mercifully spared you. That has certainly been the experience of my life.

You may even be living in open rebellion right now. Yet God, in his love and grace, is reaching out to you at this very moment. As verse 31 tells us, "Nevertheless, in your great mercies you did not make an end of them or forsake them, for you are a gracious and merciful God." What a great and compassionate God we serve!

If you have rejected God's gracious offer of salvation, if you have rebelled against the God who loves you, I want you to know that he reaches out to you from a blood-stained cross.

There have been many times in my own life when God would have had every right to say, "That's it, Michael! I'm through with you. I've had enough. I will not strive with you forever." Praise God, he has never said that to me. His mercy and compassion have never failed me.

God loves you in spite of your lukewarmness. He loves you even when you give him and his church the crumbs from your table. He loves you even when you wander into sin and rebellion. And he is waiting for you to return to him, to commit yourself totally to him, and to say, "I've had enough of my own way. Starting today, and for the rest of my life, I will follow your way, Lord."

Do you know what it means to humble yourself before the Lord? It means that you look back over your life and you see all the promises you've broken, you see all the times you've taken his grace and mercy for granted, you see all the times you've broken God's heart through your sin and rebellion—and you repent of it. You turn away from those sins, and you turn back toward God. That is humility. That is what the people of Israel did in this prayer in Nehemiah 9. Looking back over their personal history, they cried out to God, "You have been faithful, but we have been faithless. So we repent in sackcloth and dust and we commit ourselves to you."

You may wonder why the people spend so much time in this prayer talking about the past. Don't let anyone tell you that history is unimportant. History is *profoundly* important. As philosopher George Santayana observed in *The Life of Reason*, "Progress, far from consisting in change, depends on retentiveness... Those who cannot remember the past are condemned to repeat it."[14]

The people of Israel remembered their past—and they repented of it. Then they sealed a commitment to God not to repeat it.

Four cornerstones of the prayer of confession

Though I have quoted this prayer only in part, I encourage you to read it in full. This prayer challenges our tendency to pray shallow, superficial, self-centered, and human-centered prayers. When God does not answer our prayers in the way and in the timeframe that we expect, we are tempted to doubt him. But the people of Israel in Nehemiah's day approached prayer very differently. Instead of expecting God to serve them, they came humbly to God and said, "We have sinned against you. We have strayed away from you. We honor you and bless you. We commit ourselves to serving you."

The prayer of Nehemiah 9 is a God-centered prayer, not a self-centered or human-centered prayer. The focus of this prayer is not "give me" or "bless me." This prayer is focused on serving God and blessing God. Here is the conclusion of this great prayer:

> "Now, therefore, our God, the great, the mighty, and the awesome God, who keeps covenant and steadfast love, let not all the hardship seem little to you that has come upon us, upon our kings, our princes, our priests, our prophets, our fathers, and all your people, since the time of the kings of Assyria until this day. Yet you have been righteous in all that has come upon us, for you have

dealt faithfully and we have acted wickedly. Our kings, our princes, our priests, and our fathers have not kept your law or paid attention to your commandments and your warnings that you gave them. Even in their own kingdom, and amid your great goodness that you gave them, and in the large and rich land that you set before them, they did not serve you or turn from their wicked works. Behold, we are slaves this day; in the land that you gave to our fathers to enjoy its fruit and its good gifts, behold, we are slaves. And its rich yield goes to the kings whom you have set over us because of our sins. They rule over our bodies and over our livestock as they please, and we are in great distress.

"Because of all this we make a firm covenant in writing; on the sealed document are the names of our princes, our Levites, and our priests" (9:32-38).

In the closing lines of this prayer, the people acknowledge that they are in distress, living as slaves in the land God had given to them, because "our kings, our princes, our priests, and our fathers have not kept your law or paid attention to your commandments and your warnings that you gave them."

There is always a price to pay for disobedience to God. Because God is gracious, because we often seem to get away with sin for a while, we soon become complacent. We take God's grace for granted. We say to ourselves, "Well, rules are made to be broken. My sins are not that serious, especially compared to what a lot of other people do. I know I'm not obeying God as I should, but I never claimed to be perfect. I figure that God must grade on a curve, so I'll probably come out with a B-minus or C-plus on my heavenly report card."

If that is the way you think, you are making a serious mistake. You are making the same mistake the people of ancient Israel so often made. Don't expect God to deal with you any differently than he dealt with the disobedient people of Israel. When you sin, you break a sacred trust-relationship with God. You don't cease to be a Christian, but you may well destroy your usefulness to God. You become like a once-beautiful plate of Wedgwood bone china that has become chipped and is no longer fit for use as part of a formal place setting.

But if you come back to him, confessing your sin, repenting and asking forgiveness, then he is gracious and merciful. He will forgive you and restore you to service for him.

If you have fallen away from your relationship with God, then King David is your role model. He is one of the great examples of a believer who walked with God, and then sinned grievously and fractured his special relationship with the Lord—before he returned to the Lord in sorrow and repentance. In Psalm 32, David wrote about the days and nights he spent struggling under his load of guilt and unconfessed sin:

> For when I kept silent, my bones wasted away
>   through my groaning all day long.
> For day and night your hand was heavy upon me;
>   my strength was dried up as by the heat of summer.
>   (Psalm 32:3-4)

Unconfessed sin haunts us. It robs us of sleep. It robs us of our relationship with God. If you are staggering under a weight of guilt and sin right now, I urge you, I plead with you to turn to the Lord, confess your sins to him, repent, and receive his cleansing shower of grace and forgiveness.

As you pray, follow the model of the prayer of Nehemiah 9 and the four cornerstones that form the foundation of this prayer:

First cornerstone: Acknowledge your personal responsibility for sin. When you pray, take all the blame, all the responsibility on yourself. Don't make excuses. Don't shift even 10 percent of the blame to someone else. Don't blame your parents, your past, your spouse, or the society you live in. You have free will, you have made sinful choices, and you accept full responsibility for your sins.

Second cornerstone: Acknowledge God's justice. Recognize that God is holy and just, and it is his prerogative to be displeased with your sin. You have no right to demand mercy, and he has every right to withhold mercy. So, as you go to God in confession and repentance, don't demand justice. Beg for mercy.

Third cornerstone: Ask God for forgiveness in the name of Jesus. The reason we can come boldly before God's throne of grace is that Jesus has already paid the penalty for our sins. We have forgiveness in the name of Jesus.

Fourth cornerstone: Cling to God's promise of forgiveness. There may be times in your life when you remember past sins and wonder if you are truly forgiven. Satan often accuses the believer's conscience, reminding the believer of sins that God has already forgiven and forgotten. Satan does this in order to destroy our effectiveness for God. But God has promised that once he has forgiven us, we are forgiven indeed. We have his Word on it—again and again and again:

> "For I will forgive their iniquity, and I will remember their sin no more" (Jeremiah 31:34).

> For as high as the heavens are above the earth,
>   so great is his steadfast love toward those who fear
>   him;
> as far as the east is from the west,
>   so far does he remove our transgressions from us.
>   (Psalm 103:11-12)

"Come now, let us reason together, says the LORD:
  though your sins are like scarlet,
they shall be as white as snow;
  though they are red like crimson,
they shall become like wool."
                                    (Isaiah 1:18)

But if we walk in the light, as he is in the light, we have fellowship with one another, and the blood of Jesus his Son cleanses us from all sin. If we say we have no sin, we deceive ourselves, and the truth is not in us. If we confess our sins, he is faithful and just to forgive us our sins and to cleanse us from all unrighteousness (1 John 1:7-9).

So go to your knees and pray the prayer of confession, repentance, and commitment. Then accept the freedom of his forgiveness and live boldly, confidently, and joyfully for him.

9

Walking on the Wall

The name *Jerusalem* means "dwelling of peace." Long before the birth of Abraham, Jerusalem was founded as a fortified city by the Jebusites, a Canaanite people. Around 1000 BC, King David laid siege to the city, which was then called Jebus. He conquered the city, and then moved the capital of Israel from Hebron to the newly conquered Jerusalem. David extended the walls and expanded the size of the city. His son and successor, King Solomon, built the first temple in the city and also extended the city walls.

King Nebuchadnezzar destroyed the city and temple in 587 BC and deported a vast number of Judean Jews to Babylon. King Cyrus II of Persia allowed the Jews to return to Judah, and sometime later, King Artaxerxes of Persia allowed Nehemiah to return to Jerusalem to rebuild the city's walls and govern the province, which remained under control of the Persian Empire.

The walls of Jerusalem that were rebuilt in Nehemiah's day were still standing during the time of Jesus of Nazareth. When the Messiah rode into Jerusalem on a donkey on that first Palm Sunday, he passed through one of the gates that had been rebuilt five centuries earlier under the leadership of Nehemiah. But in AD 70, about four decades after Jesus entered Jerusalem as the King of the Jews, the walls were leveled by forces commanded by the Roman general Titus (who would later rule as Roman emperor from 79 to 81). A Roman colony, Aelia Capitolina, was later built on the ruins of Jerusalem. The Crusaders captured the city in 1099, and Muslim forces under Saladin, the first Sultan of Egypt and Syria, conquered the city in 1187.

If you visit the old city of Jerusalem today, the walls you see date back to the era of the Ottoman Sultan Suleiman the Magnificent. Those walls were built from 1535 to 1538. The Jerusalem walls of Nehemiah's time are long gone.

That is the historical perspective as we come to this closing section of the book of Nehemiah, chapters 10 through 13. In Nehemiah 9, we saw the great prayer of the Jewish people—a prayer of confession and commitment.

We will summarize Nehemiah 10 briefly, because this chapter consists primarily of two lists: First, it lists the names of the people who sealed the covenant prayer of Nehemiah 9. Second, it lists the obligations the people took upon themselves as signers and keepers of the covenant.

And we will summarize Nehemiah 11 in the same way. This chapter is a list of the leaders in Jerusalem—the city leaders, the leaders of the province and nearby towns, the Levites, the priests, the temple servants, the gatekeepers, and so forth. Nehemiah 11 also lists the nearby villages outside of Jerusalem.

Nehemiah 12 opens with a list of priests and Levites, then it goes on to tell the story of the dedication of the wall and the renewed service at the temple. We will focus our attention on this chapter.

Nehemiah 13 deals with events that take place a dozen years after the rebuilding of the walls. After governing Judah for a time, Nehemiah returns to Susa in Persia where he continues to serve King Artaxerxes for twelve more years. Then he requests leave to return to Jerusalem. On his return, he discovers that the people have backslidden from their commitment to God. They have stopped financially supporting the Levites. They are profaning the Sabbath and intermarrying with pagans in violation of God's Law. The temple priest, Eliashib, has allowed Tobiah the Ammonite to occupy a room in the temple—another violation of God's Law. So Nehemiah cleanses the temple and institutes reforms among the people.

As the book of Nehemiah closes, we see once again that the human heart is prone to wander from God and his Law. Godly leaders must continually be on guard against apostasy in themselves and in the people they lead. Nehemiah exemplifies godly leadership, and in the end, the walls of the city stand strong, the evildoers have been punished, and the spiritual vitality of Jerusalem has been renewed. Nehemiah concludes with this prayer, "Remember me, O my God, for good."

Now let's take a closer look at Nehemiah 12 and the dedication of the wall.

A day of celebration

Turning to the middle of Nehemiah 12, we see the people of God gathering to dedicate the recently completed wall. It is a time of praise and joyous celebration:

> And at the dedication of the wall of Jerusalem they sought the Levites in all their places, to bring them to

> Jerusalem to celebrate the dedication with gladness, with
> thanksgivings and with singing, with cymbals, harps, and
> lyres. And the sons of the singers gathered together from
> the district surrounding Jerusalem and from the villages
> of the Netophathites; also from Beth-gilgal and from the
> region of Geba and Azmaveth, for the singers had built
> for themselves villages around Jerusalem. And the priests
> and the Levites purified themselves, and they purified the
> people and the gates and the wall (12:27-30).

The people of Israel have endured decades of humiliation and defeat. They have gone through a long time of exile, and they have mourned their shattered city. But they have also gone through a time of restoration and renewal, and now it is time to celebrate.

Israel's spiritual identity and national identity have been restored. The spirit of the Jewish people has been revived. They have received a new sense of vision. It's time to rejoice and be happy again. It's time to celebrate the presence and the power of God.

This is what every Sunday morning worship service in every Bible-believing church should be like—a time of celebration and rejoicing. It should be a time when we not only commemorate the death of the Lord Jesus, but we also celebrate the resurrection and the empty tomb.

The reason we gather together on Sunday mornings to worship the Lord is that the first day of the week is Resurrection Day. Sunday reminds us in words and symbols that we have been ransomed from sin and we are redeemed. It reminds us that we are heirs of the living God. It reminds us that if we have been buried with Christ, we shall be raised with Christ. It reminds us that we live in this world but we do not belong to this world. It reminds us that we are pilgrims on our way to heaven.

Every other day of the week may be like Good Friday, full of trials, pain, and defeat. But Resurrection Day is a day of rejoicing. The great preacher and evangelist Charles Haddon Spurgeon once told a group of pastors, "When you speak of heaven, let your face light up, let it be irradiated with a heavenly gleam, let your eyes shine with reflected glory. But when you speak of hell, well, your ordinary face will do."

Here in Nehemiah 12, it seems that the people have heaven on their minds. We read that the people came to Jerusalem "to celebrate the dedication with gladness, with thanksgivings and with singing, with cymbals, harps, and lyres." The Jewish people are an expressive, emotional people. When they bring out the instruments and they start the music, you know they are going to have a party. You know there will be a noisy celebration and an uninhibited good time. This was going down in history as a memorable day—the day they dedicated Jerusalem's new wall to the Lord.

A day of purification

But there was also a serious dimension to their celebration. We also read, "And the priests and the Levites purified themselves, and they purified the people and the gates and the wall."

Before the celebration, there must be purification. Before a time of joy, there must be confession. Before there can be peace with God, the peace that passes understanding, there must be repentance and a commitment to walk in obedience. The Scriptures tell us that the priests purified themselves and the people, and they purified the gates and the wall. There was a ceremony or rite of purification.

Though this passage doesn't tell us what that ceremony consisted of, from other portions of Scripture we can determine that it probably involved a sin offering. Before you can truly celebrate the resurrection, before you can truly celebrate the presence of God, before you can experience true joy, your heart must be purified. Holiness precedes happiness. Cleansing precedes celebration.

Before I can minister to anyone else, I must have a clean heart and clean hands. I must be cleansed by the power of the Holy Spirit before I have anything of eternal value to offer anyone else.

We can't fake a clean heart and a clean conscience. Many people try to do so and appear to succeed for a while—but as Spurgeon also wisely said, "God will not allow his children to sin successfully." God won't let us get away with sweeping our sins under the rug and pretending to be clean. Phony cleansing will always fail. Phony saints are always exposed sooner or later. Phony righteousness was the very sin that Jesus opposed most vehemently when he clashed with the hypocritical scribes and Pharisees.

Don't let moral carelessness, so-called "little sins," steal your joy in the Lord and destroy your usefulness to him. If you wonder why the Christian life has lost its appeal, if you wonder why your laughter rings hollow in your ears, if you wonder why you feel you have nothing to celebrate in the Christian life, perhaps it's because you've been trying to laugh off the very sins that God hates.

If you want to experience the joy of the Lord, then it's time to come clean with God. It's time to confess and repent and make a new commitment of obedience to him. Don't waste another day wandering away from him. Turn from your sin, run to God, and celebrate a joyous reunion with him.

One of the greatest statements ever penned on human rights is this sentence from the Declaration of Independence: "We hold these truths to be self-evident, that all men are created equal, that they are endowed by their Creator with certain unalienable Rights, that among these are Life, Liberty and the pursuit of Happiness." It is absolutely right and fitting that all humans should be treated as equal and should be free to live their lives, enjoy the blessings of liberty, and pursue happiness in any way they choose.

And there is no question that America is a happiness-pursuing nation. Unfortunately, most people pursue happiness with almost a sense of desperation. People are killing themselves in their quest for riches, fame, sexual pleasure, entertainment, drugs, and on and on. And one of the great tragedies of this life is that so many people pursue happiness in the wrong ways, in the wrong places, and in the wrong values. They fail to realize that God is the only One who can truly make us happy.

If happiness could be found in wealth and things, most people in America would be delirious with joy. Instead, America is afflicted with high rates of suicide, depression, child abuse, divorce, and a host of other ills. If Nehemiah could address America today, I believe his message might be, "If you want to have true happiness, if you want to have something worth celebrating, come clean with God. Confess your sin, repent, and commit your ways to him."

Jumping on the wall

Once the people of Israel had come clean before God, Nehemiah led the leaders of the people up onto the wall:

> Then I brought the leaders of Judah up onto the wall and appointed two great choirs that gave thanks. One went to the south on the wall to the Dung Gate. And after them went Hoshaiah and half of the leaders of Judah, and Azariah, Ezra, Meshullam, Judah, Benjamin, Shemaiah, and Jeremiah, and certain of the priests' sons with trumpets: Zechariah the son of Jonathan, son of Shemaiah, son of Mattaniah, son of Micaiah, son of

> Zaccur, son of Asaph; and his relatives, Shemaiah, Azarel, Milalai, Gilalai, Maai, Nethanel, Judah, and Hanani, with the musical instruments of David the man of God. And Ezra the scribe went before them. At the Fountain Gate they went up straight before them by the stairs of the city of David, at the ascent of the wall, above the house of David, to the Water Gate on the east (12:31-37).

Once they were on the wall, Nehemiah appointed two great choirs to sing hymns of thanks to God. I can't help picturing Nehemiah as a bold, emotional, exuberant man, full of the joy of life. I can picture him up on the wall, leading those two choirs, clapping his hands, leaping with praise, maybe even tap-dancing—and calling for the other leaders to come up on the wall and join him. I can even picture Nehemiah *jumping up and down* on the wall. Why? Remember this scene from Nehemiah 4:

> Now when Sanballat heard that we were building the wall, he was angry and greatly enraged, and he jeered at the Jews. And he said in the presence of his brothers and of the army of Samaria, "What are these feeble Jews doing? Will they restore it for themselves? Will they sacrifice? Will they finish up in a day? Will they revive the stones out of the heaps of rubbish, and burned ones at that?" Tobiah the Ammonite was beside him, and he said, "Yes, what they are building—if a fox goes up on it he will break down their stone wall!" (4:1-3).

Sanballat, Tobiah, and Geshem opposed Nehemiah and tried to derail the rebuilding project at every step along the way. They used mockery, trickery, threats, intimidation, and manipulation—but every one of their efforts failed utterly because God was with

Nehemiah. All the people heard Sanballat's mockery. They heard Tobiah claim that the wall would collapse if a fox scampered across it. It's easy to imagine Nehemiah jumping up and down on the wall, saying, "How about that, Sanballat? How about that, Tobiah? I'm a lot bigger than a fox—and the wall still stands! And why is this wall standing? Because God built it!"

Nehemiah 12:31 tells us that one choir got up on the top of the wall and moved toward the Dung Gate at the southern end of the city. Then, in verse 38, the second choir went north, followed by Nehemiah:

> The other choir of those who gave thanks went to the north, and I followed them with half of the people, on the wall, above the Tower of the Ovens, to the Broad Wall, and above the Gate of Ephraim, and by the Gate of Yeshanah, and by the Fish Gate and the Tower of Hananel and the Tower of the Hundred, to the Sheep Gate; and they came to a halt at the Gate of the Guard. So both choirs of those who gave thanks stood in the house of God, and I and half of the officials with me; and the priests Eliakim, Maaseiah, Miniamin, Micaiah, Elioenai, Zechariah, and Hananiah, with trumpets; and Maaseiah, Shemaiah, Eleazar, Uzzi, Jehohanan, Malchijah, Elam, and Ezer. And the singers sang with Jezrahiah as their leader. And they offered great sacrifices that day and rejoiced, for God had made them rejoice with great joy; the women and children also rejoiced. And the joy of Jerusalem was heard far away (12:38-43).

Imagine this scene: Nehemiah, the leaders of the people, and two great choirs are up on the wall, singing and dancing and praising God. When we see the word *choirs*, we tend to think of church choirs dressed in flowing white robes, standing in rows in the choir loft. That, of course, does not describe the two choirs that sang from the walls of Jerusalem that day.

Imagine, instead, an exuberant gospel choir—hands raised, tambourines shaking, feet dancing, voices shouting, the stone wall shaking from the vibrations of that joyful noise and those dancing feet. Here's how Nehemiah describes the scene: "And they offered great sacrifices that day and rejoiced, for God had made them rejoice with great joy; the women and children also rejoiced. And the joy of Jerusalem was heard far away."

The joy was heard far away!

Have you ever been in a packed football stadium or a sold-out basketball arena during a big game? Do you remember the roar of the crowd and the brassy sound of the band? Then you may have some idea of the excitement that shook the city of Jerusalem that day.

That's what Christian celebration should look like and sound like. When we celebrate before the Lord, we should sing to him and focus on his presence with us. We should shout and rejoice. We should offer great sacrifices to him—and I don't mean we should sacrifice animals. Today we sacrifice to the Lord by passing the collection plate and giving sacrificially to his work.

"Make a joyful noise"

Picture the parade that passed along the top of the city wall that day. Imagine the procession of people, some singing, some blowing trumpets, while others danced and shouted and celebrated around the city. It was a parade to end all parades—so exuberant, so joyful it would make the Rose Parade or a Disneyland parade look like a funeral procession by comparison.

The people of Jerusalem were not merely celebrating. They were serving notice on the devil: "Satan, keep your sourpuss friends away from here. This is a rejoicing zone, and there's no room in this city for a Sanballat, a Tobiah, or a Geshem. We are rejoicing and praising our God!"

Do you experience this kind of rejoicing in your own Christian life? If not, why not? Exuberant, uninhibited, joyful praise should mark our worship and thanksgiving to God. As the psalmist wrote:

> Oh come, let us sing to the LORD;
>   let us make a joyful noise to the rock of our
>   salvation!
> Let us come into his presence with thanksgiving;
>   let us make a joyful noise to him with songs of
>   praise!
>   (Psalm 95:1-2)

Christian, if you are a dour, prune-faced, tightlipped worshiper, my message to you is…lighten up! Sing to the Lord! Make a joyful noise to the rock of your salvation! Joyful hearts are contagious. Wherever you are, express your joy and spread some joy to other hearts around you.

When I was in seminary, I was not merely poor. I had nothing— not figuratively but literally nothing. I was able to attend seminary purely by the grace of God. In that place, we had hot and cold running rats. The conditions were difficult, and I look back on my seminary days with great fondness. Why? Because the joy of the Lord filled the place. In that seminary, I experienced Christian love, fellowship, praise, singing, and the excitement and anticipation of preparing for future ministry.

One time, during the week of exams, I was walking through the single students' quarters. I had a room there where I did my late-night studies. As I walked through the quadrangle, I was singing praise songs to the Lord. It was during the summer, it was a hot evening, and all the students had their windows open for some fresh air as they studied. As I walked and sang, I heard voices from a few windows calling, "Here comes Youssef!"—along with assorted complaints about my singing. But I didn't care. I felt like Nehemiah, shouting and rejoicing on his brand-new wall, and no amount of ribbing from my fellow students could keep me from singing.

A few days later, I learned that one of the students in those quarters was struggling with his studies. He was discouraged and ready to throw in the towel. But he heard me singing as I walked through the quadrangle, and he said to himself, "If that Egyptian immigrant can study these subjects that I'm studying and can still be this joyful—then surely I can succeed here as well."

My joy turned out to be contagious. Though I didn't find out until later, this fellow student drew encouragement from my joyful noise. He successfully completed his studies and today he is an effective pastor, serving the Lord.

If you feel like singing (and every genuine believer should experience this kind of joy daily), don't hold it in. Sing! Make a joyful noise! Don't let anyone or anything keep you from singing praise to the Lord.

Think of all the people who are within your sphere of influence—the people in your family, your neighborhood, your office, your campus, your military unit. Many of them are lonely and desperate. Think of what your songs of joy would mean to them. Think of the opportunity for witness it would give you when they say, "What makes you so happy? Why are you always singing?"

It may not always be appropriate to sing songs of praise and joy. But you can still go around with a smile on your face and the light of the Lord in your eyes and a message of cheer and grace on your lips. A simple attitude of cheerfulness, especially when people know you are going through difficult circumstances, speaks volumes about your Christian faith without you ever having to say a word. It tells the people around you that your happiness is not dependent on your circumstances. It tells people that you can be happy even amid trials and problems—because your joy comes from the Lord, not from your circumstances.

The late evangelical theologian Francis Schaeffer put it this way: "When we understand our calling, it is not only true, but beautiful—and it should be exciting. It is hard to understand how an orthodox, evangelical, Bible-believing Christian can fail to be excited…If we are unexcited Christians, we should go back and see what is wrong."[15]

If you aren't experiencing the joy and excitement of the Lord right now, I urge you to deal with that issue before you close this book. If you have never received Jesus as your Lord and Savior, you can do so right now. If you are already a Christian, but you have wandered away from God, you can come clean with him right now. Confess your sins, repent, and return to him, and commit to living in obedience to him. You can start today, this very moment. Whether you are coming to Christ for the first time or coming back to him to renew your commitment, you can pray a prayer like this one:

> Father in heaven, I confess to you that I am a sinner. I'm sorry for my sins, and I repent of them and turn away from them. I invite Jesus to come into my life, to be Lord of my life, and to take control of my life. Please seal this

decision I've made and help me to live faithfully every day for you. Thank you for hearing my prayer. In Jesus's name, amen.

If that is truly the prayer of your heart right now, the Lord will receive you. He will make you clean. He will fill you with joy and gladness. He will blot out your sins and create a clean heart within you. He will fill you with his Holy Spirit and restore to you the joy of your salvation.

If the walls of your life are broken today, let him come in and clear away the wreckage and rubble of your past. Let him rebuild the walls of your family, your relationships, and your world. Let him restore you and transform your life into a Jerusalem, a "dwelling of peace."

Notes

1. Kerby Anderson, ed., *Technology, Spirituality, and Social Trends: Probing the Headlines That Impact Your Family* (Grand Rapids, MI: Kregel, 2002), 112-13.

2. You may be wondering why one of the gates in the Jerusalem city wall is called the Dung Gate. Bible historians believe it was named for the animal droppings removed from the temple area, the result of having so many sacrificial animals there. The droppings were taken from the temple area, carted through the Dung Gate, and dumped in the Valley of Hinnom, where they were burned.

3. John C. Maxwell, *Be a People Person: Effective Leadership Through Effective Relationships* (Colorado Springs, CO: David C. Cook, 2007), 95.

4. Ann Landers, "Dear Ann Landers: Rose Has to Go," *Daily News* (Bowling Green, KY), February 17, 1986, 5.

5. Chaplain (Lt. Col.) Donald Eubank, "Cooperation Is a Key to Success," *Hawaii Army Weekly*, September 17, 2012, www.hawaiiarmyweekly.com/2012/09/17/cooperation-is-a-key-to-success/.

6. Ann Dunnewold, *Even June Cleaver Would Forget the Juice Box* (Deerfield Beach, FL: Health Communications, Inc., 2007), 69-70.

7. Nick Spark, *A History of Murphy's Law* (Los Angeles: Nick Spark, 2006), 24-25.

8. Drew Zahn, "Questioning Faith of Same-Sex 'Marriage' Fans 'Bulls—'" WorldNetDaily.com, May 18, 2013, www.wnd.com/2013/05/questioning-faith-of-same-sex-marriage-fans-bulls/; Nicola Menzie, "Rob Bell Grows Frustrated Amid Questions on 'Sinfulness' of Homosexuality," *The Christian Post*, May 4, 2013, www.christianpost.com/news/rob-bell-grows-frustrated-amid-questions-on-sinfulness-of-homosexuality-95209/; "Rob Bell and Andrew Wilson//Homosexuality and the Bible//Unbelievable?," May 3, 2013, www.youtube.com/watch?feature=player_embedded&v=XF9uo_P0nNI.

9. Ayn Rand, *Atlas Shrugged* (New York: Penguin, 1999), 411.

10. Haddon W. Robinson, "Money Matters," *Our Daily Bread*, May 20, 2005, http://odb.beta.rbc.org/2005/05/20/money-matters/.

11. Iron Eyes Cody, "You Knew What I Was," *Guideposts*, June 1990, 5-7, reprinted by *TeacherAide*, www.inquest.org/ss/ta/tfe1-5.htm.

12. Robert Strand, *Moments for Each Other: Warm Remembrances of Your Time Together* (Oak Grove, AR: New Leaf Press, 1994), entry for Day 29, "Need to Be Hugged."

13. H.A. Ironside, *Illustrations of Bible Truth* (Chicago: Moody Press, 1945), 104-6; dialogue paraphrased for clearer understanding by today's readers.

14. George Santayana, *The Life of Reason*, vol. 1 (1905), www.gutenberg.org/files/15000/15000 -h/15000-h.htm.

15. Francis A. Schaeffer, *The God Who Is There* (Downers Grove, IL: InterVarsity Press, 1998), 190.

About the Author

Michael Youssef, PhD, is the founder and president of Leading The Way, a worldwide ministry that leads the way for people living in spiritual darkness to discover the light of Christ through the creative use of media and on-the-ground ministry teams. His weekly television programs and daily radio programs are broadcast more than 4300 times per week in 25 languages to more than 190 countries. He is also the founding pastor of The Church of The Apostles in Atlanta, Georgia.

Dr. Youssef was born in Egypt and lived in Lebanon and Australia before coming to the United States. In 1984, he fulfilled his childhood dream of becoming an American citizen. He holds degrees from Moore College in Sydney, Australia, and Fuller Theological Seminary in California. In 1984, he earned a PhD in social anthropology from Emory University. He and his wife reside in Atlanta and have four grown children and eight grandchildren.

For more on Michael Youssef, The Church of The Apostles, and Leading The Way, visit apostles.org and www.leadingtheway.org.

To learn more about Harvest House books and
to read sample chapters, visit our website:

www.harvesthousepublishers.com

HARVEST HOUSE PUBLISHERS
EUGENE, OREGON